X vs. Y

A CULTURE WAR,
A LOVE STORY

EVE EPSTEIN   AND   LEONORA EPSTEIN

ABRAMS IMAGE, NEW YORK

CONTENTS

X VS. Y: WHICH IS WHICH?

ASK GOOGLE WHICH BIRTH YEARS DEFINE GEN X OR GEN Y, AND YOU'LL COME UP WITH A LOT OF DIFFERENT ANSWERS. IN OUR CONVERSATIONS, WE'VE TENDED TO TREAT GEN X AS FOLKS BORN IN THE MID-SIXTIES TO LATE SEVENTIES AND MILLENNIALS/GEN YERS AS PEOPLE BORN AROUND THE EARLY EIGHTIES TO THE LATE NINETIES. IN SPEAKING WITH FRIENDS OF BOTH GENERATIONS, WE FOUND A DISTINCT GRAY AREA WHERE PEOPLE BORN BETWEEN 1979 AND 1984 OR SO FELT EITHER THAT THEY WERE MEMBERS OF NEITHER GENERATION OR THAT THEY WERE IN A POSITION TO CHOOSE. MOST IN THAT POSITION CHOSE TO IDENTIFY WITH GEN X, BECAUSE WHEN GIVEN THE CHOICE BETWEEN DOC MARTENS AND FOAM FOOTWEAR, THE CHOICE SEEMS OBVIOUS.

DON'T MESS WITH X'S

One of the many, many, many terrible things that happen when you get older is that you find yourself earnestly saying things you used to say in jest. Things like "I just don't understand what the kids are wearing these days." Or "What ever happened to *manners*?" Or "Could you turn that down?"

These outbursts of stodgy grown-upness are made weirder in my case by the fact that they're addressed not to a bunch of nameless neighborhood hooligans but to my sister, Leonora, who happens to be fourteen years younger than I am. It's a comeuppance I richly deserve for subjecting her to the unsavory predilections of my own Gen-X youth. She will likely never forget the disembowelingly loud Jesus Lizard show I dragged her to at the age of twelve (more on that later) or the time I shocked her to tears with my newly platinum hair or the parade of boyfriends whose dubious fashion choices ranged from Pocahontas braids to split-toe Nikes to the full late-seventies polyester regalia commonly associated with the Ernie/Bert crowd. And so the price I pay for all that is to hear myself grousing, grumpy-old-man-style, at her generation's breezy penchant for casual sex or their upstart ways in the workplace or their inexplicable nostalgia for Jonathan Taylor Thomas.

That's a big part of the reason I wanted to write this book with her: I wanted to hear, from her, what she loves about her generation, what she thinks makes them special. I wanted her take on the ideas, movies, books, and technologies that they love, and to know which of them helped make her who she is today. Because for all my grousing, I can't deny that she's grown up to be a pretty impressive person. She's smart and funny and well rounded and understands Twitter a lot better than I do. And she's not the only one: Some of my best friends are Gen Yers. They're tolerant, enthusiastic, energetic, opinionated, and ambitious, and I expect they have a thing or two to teach the rest of us—if only we'll stop complaining about how entitled they all seem for a minute.

Which is not, obviously, to say they're better than us. The other reason I wanted to write this book was to explore the ways in which my generation is awesome. Which can be scary—not because we're *not* awesome, but

Millennials have a capacity for feeling nostalgia for things we can't actually lay claim to, and so we steal heavily from Gen X's pool of awesomeness, cultivating extensive vinyl collections and obscure Pixies trivia knowledge. On the less cool side, we spearhead "ironic" revivals of fashions that shouldn't have happened a first time—fanny packs, Sally Jesse Raphael glasses, neon spandex. I'm really sorry for all that, but that's not the point. The point is that Gen Y couldn't exist without Gen X because we've (selectively) made their nostalgia our nostalgia.

This might have something to do with the fact that members of Gen Y are still evolving, growing up, and trying to figure which of our own collective memories we want to preserve (hello, *Fraggle Rock*) and which we want to quietly discard on history's scrap heap (adios, the Macarena). When I started writing this book, these cultural conversations were footnotes when it came to talking about my generation. The larger discussion was about how we're all screwed and either living in our parents' basements, begging for internships, or having impossibly awesome careers, working in offices with beer pong in the conference room and twenty-five-year-old CEOs. We've been characterized as either entitled, delusional overachievers, or basement-dwelling victims of a crappy economy. Failures or brats. Don't get me wrong: This conversation is still happening and will be an unfortunate part of our story, but in a matter of months, our identity shifted because the "child of the nineties" talk exploded. So, now we're all pop-culture addicts who can't get enough of old Bagel Bites commercials on YouTube.

We tend to talk about these things in self-deprecating tones because a lot of this stuff is downright bad and embarrassing—kind of like our pasts have been doused in Nickelodeon green slime (this is actually more probable than not). Yes, you might reminisce about the most important film of your youth—*Titanic,* obviously—but it's way cooler to say that your favorite movie is *Heathers*.

So it's natural that we'd be struggling to define ourselves—both in our own right and in relation to those who came before us. And so the desire to represent Gen Y in this inevitable culture war/love story with Gen X is a big reason I wanted to write this book.

Well, that, and all the good jobs were taken. Thanks a lot, Mark Zuckerberg.

NIRVANA

DURAN DURAN

PIXIES

R.E.M.

GUNS N' ROSES

A TRIBE CALLED QUEST

MADONNA

BJÖRK

BEASTIE BOYS

NO DOUBT

BRITNEY SPEARS

VAMPIRE WEEKEND

DESTINY'S CHILD

MGMT

CHAPTER 1
MUSIC

———

X MUSIC INTRO

X, DRUGS, AND ROCK 'N' ROLL

Growing up, I thought "Good Vibrations" was the jingle for Sunkist oranges. I had no idea that it'd had a whole respectable previous life as a real song, one that young people had previously listened to without envisioning impossibly shiny citrus fruit glistening in the white-hot Florida sun. I had no idea what that song represented to the people who first embraced it, no inkling of the horror they must have felt watching that commercial.

Back before Pandemic and Spotitunes made all music equally available in exactly the same way, how we heard a band or a song was much less up to us. We heard it on the radio, or on TV, or, in the very beginning, we simply listened to the records that just happened to be in the house. Hence the first popular music I remember hearing was the following, in no particular order: the Beatles' *Abbey Road*, the *Saturday Night Fever* soundtrack, ABBA's *Gold: Greatest Hits*, *The Best of Blondie*, and Melissa Manchester's *Melissa*, which featured, among other gems, "Stevie's Wonder," a stirring funk-by-way-of-adult-contemporary tribute. (This last influence came not, strictly speaking, from inside the house but across the hall: Believe it or not, Melissa Manchester was our next-door neighbor.)

It's likely that I was the only person in the world listening to all of these artists with equal satisfaction; looking back, those were heady times, perhaps the only period in my life when the songs I loved were mine alone and not part of some larger cultural landscape in which I was trying to find my place. By this I mean that my generation inherited its ideas about music from the sixties and seventies, when popular music and subcultures were knitted together inextricably and what you listened to defined not only the songs on your personal soundtrack but also the clothes you wore, the people you hung out with, and your political views. Disco and rock, folk and country, metal and prog rock, new wave and punk: Each had its following, and each defined a particular worldview, and those worldviews were more often incompatible than not.

The idea that a whole mini-cultural movement could be built around the statement "Disco sucks" or "Die, hippies" is hard, I think, for people of Generation Y to grasp: To them, music is just what you listen to, not what you are. They might enjoy a mix that includes everything from Carly Rae Jepsen to Bon Iver and not be considered inconsistent; for us, it's a little different. We identify with our rock gods, with our fellow fans, and with the "ideas" or sensibilities they represent.

At some point in my life, I learned to have two musical identities: the outward-facing, Gen X–aligned one that broadcast my love for "cool" bands like Pavement, the Pixies, Dinosaur Jr., the Beatles, the Beastie Boys, X, R.E.M., A Tribe Called Quest, and De La Soul; and my private self, which indulged in guilty pleasures like Madonna, Mariah Carey, George Michael, and Barry Manilow. No matter how much I see the world around me changing—watch punk rock signifiers get hollowed out by teen pop stars or people who look like ravers listening to Johnny Cash—I still hold on to those old categories of cool and not cool, subculture A vs. subculture B (or vs. mainstream culture), and stand in judgment of the part of me that loves a song for its own sake. The idea that I don't have to be embarrassed by the rather large offering of Olivia Newton-John songs in my iTunes library is one I have trouble accepting.

I will therefore continue to observe this antiquated public/private split: I will keep my Spotify feed private and dance like no one's watching only when no one really is watching. Which isn't to say I don't love the "cool" bands as well; but with those bands, there will always be other dynamics at play, dynamics of coolness, of newness, of indie cred and selling out (all issues Olivia Newton-John never had to contend with). While the uncool artists were always mine in some private way, the cool ones were "ours" collectively. And as such, how much you actually liked the music was only part of why you loved the band; you loved what it said about you, what the band represented, and what it inspired, something that brought us together or drove us apart, inspired feelings of fierce loyalty or even violent outrage when somehow desecrated or misrepresented—much like my parents' generation must have felt when watching that Sunkist commercial.

Which gets at the thing I think is probably true for all generations: Generally speaking, when it comes to the music you cherish, it's best to remember that anything terrible you can imagine, and a great number of terrible things you can't, will almost certainly happen eventually. Someone will ruin a great song with a terrible cover of it. Someone will mash up your two least favorite songs to make your new least favorite song. Someone will put an Iggy Pop song into a Carnival Cruise ad. Someone will destroy a good movie with a terrible song or a great song with a terrible movie. Someone will turn seventy and still wear spandex on tour. Someone will tell you the Beatles were overrated. Someone will commit suicide. You will be disappointed, horrified, irritated, aggrieved. And yet you will forge on, swimming against the cold, pitiless tide of culture and clinging to what you first loved in the music and musicians you love. And then you'll know which ones really mattered all along.

Y MUSIC INTRO

NOW THAT'S WHAT WE CALL MUSIC

Y Chumbawamba have just split up. It is July 2012, and the way the news has gone viral online, you'd think Gen Y has gone into a state of deep mourning. All of a sudden, we seem to care about the British band Americans know for one song only, a horrible, dude-y, football-esque (or "soccer," to normal people) 1997 hit called "Tubthumping." As soon as the "Tubthumping" hype turned to hate (it didn't take long), Chumbawamba fell off the radar completely.

But now that they're really gone after an apparent three-decade career (I know, crazy), we feel an ironic sorrow for some nineties memories that now somehow seem iconic.

Taken objectively, the body of musical work produced during Gen Y's formative years isn't exactly an example of creative brilliance. But we're beginning to understand and experience a phenomenon that happens so universally—that distance yields genius. This is not to say that we now consider "Tubthumping" to be some musical masterpiece. (We're not *that* dumb.) But while *Billboard*-topping acts like Britney, Smash Mouth, the Spice Girls, SisQó, Ace of Base, and Barenaked Ladies rank nowhere near in caliber to, say, the Beatles, they're all important in their own ways, or at least more kindly considered, thanks to an ample dose of nostalgia.

This may be because our nostalgia isn't just about the songs. It's about an era in which the music industry was still hanging on to an old-school model before Napster would come along and desecrate it, *Independence Day* style. As our generation began bridging the gap from physical to digital, we realized that we'd also be the last group to experience a predigital music industry.

We began consuming music under highly controlled conditions. Information was fed directly to you through *TRL* or other mainstream media sources, and then it was up to you to acquire and keep information, which was valuable. Your CD collection was, after all, a representation of your allowance. It was also a physical embodiment of how cool you were.

As for me, I found myself forming three different relationships to music in my pre-mp3 days. There was my mainstream catalog, which included the stuff that everyone listened to. These were largely teen pop singers and boy bands—Christina Aguilera, Britney Spears, Mandy Moore, Backstreet Boys. The type of music emblematic of fantasy Hollywood lives. The kind of catchy tunes meant to be shared at school dances and slumber parties. The kind of driving-in-a-car-with-your-girlfriends music that made you feel like *this is our moment* and you'd almost see things in slow motion.

Then there were soundtracks. The *Romeo + Juliet* soundtrack was and will forever remain huge for Gen Y. Some other notable favorites: *Titanic, She's All That*, and *The Wedding Singer*. (Ironically, my introduction to eighties music would come from that last soundtrack, and it took me years to realize that "Rapper's Delight" doesn't actually feature a rapping eighty-year-old woman.) The tracks on these compilations would be tied to movie images and fictional moments, oftentimes involving imaginary makeout sessions with Leonardo DiCaprio, Ryan Phillippe, Skeet Ulrich, or Freddie Prinze Jr. On these discs were songs that hypnotized, causing you to replay fairy-tale scenes. Think daydreamy ballads like Sixpence None the Richer's "Kiss Me" or the infamous "My Heart Will Go On"—the melodies that drive an adolescent girl to wax poetic on love and life in countless diary entries.

But most valuable to me in that library wasn't the stuff handed over by *YM* or Carson Daly. It was the stuff you had to *discover* (which I knew was infinitely cooler), largely gifts created by Gen X musicians or handed down to me by Gen Xers: Liz Phair, Elliott Smith, Nirvana, Beck, the Smiths, R.E.M.,

Radiohead, Pavement, the Cranberries, Everything But the Girl. Kind of mysteriously, these groups hinted at a world I'd eventually get to be a part of. This world was outside my bedroom, but far from MTV, and included unbelievably cool people who sat around listening to this same exact CD. I wanted to go to there.

I finally got to there around the time I started college, but by then things were rapidly changing. For a while there was a genius program called MyTunes that let you essentially copy and paste songs from any iTunes library on a shared network. It was *awesome*. There was so much out there, and we were obsessed with acquiring all of it, fattening up our iTunes libraries to hold days', weeks', and then months' worth of music. I downloaded everything with a name I'd heard of and then downloaded anything with a name that sounded cool (which would account for my extensive collection of Sun Ra). The rate of discovery at this point increased dramatically, and music really began to lose its tangibility. Instead, we found ourselves having this new and amazing advantage of getting to know a new indie group like the Shins or hear the latest Belle & Sebastian album without having to wait for it to make its rounds to us.

Over the years, the result has turned music into a huge, shared thing that exists around you more than it defines you. Instead of *discovering*, we're *pulling* from "clouds" and all sorts of different sources. The accessibility has allowed us to broaden our musical tastes, but it's also given us a shorter attention span. A perfect example might be Gotye's 2011 album, *Making Mirrors*. Gotye was, for lack of a better word, what you'd call an "indie" artist. His hit, "Somebody That I Used to Know," enjoyed a brief stint as a hipster anthem.

It was a beautiful song with soulful vocals. Until all of a sudden it sucked.

In the blink of an eye, a little bit of good was enough to catapult Gotye to mass status. The idea of someone like Gotye having the number-one album in America would have been sheer lunacy in 1999. But now popular tastes have shifted to include things that should be niche.

It's unlikely that Gotye will come to belong in the same class of obsolete, one-hit, mediocre bands like Chumbawamba. But then again, that's what we said about John Mayer. If only we could have had the foresight to see that "Your Body Is a Wonderland" is so not.

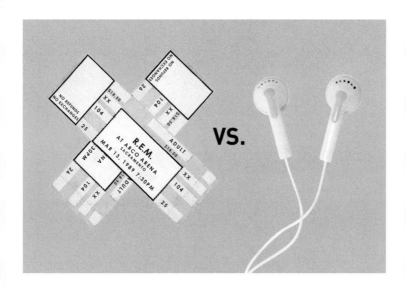

MIX MESSAGES

A mix is a musical snapshot, a form of communication, commemoration, and self-expression. We have no idea how Third Eye Blind would feel about sharing a playlist with Ace of Base, but that's kind of the point: It's how we make their music ours, liberating each song from the artist's intentions and attaching our own, personal meaning to it, and to the whole, which becomes a personal soundtrack.

GEN X MUSIC MIXES

ONE-NIGHT STANDARDS

Van Halen, Jamie's Cryin'
Liz Phair, Fuck and Run
The Replacements, If Only You Were Lonely
Duran Duran, Save a Prayer
Prince, Darling Nikki
Foreigner, Hot Blooded
Michael Jackson, Dirty Diana
Squeeze, Tempted
Pat Benatar, Hit Me with Your Best Shot
Faces, Stay with Me
Tina Turner, Private Dancer
Bon Jovi, You Give Love a Bad Name
INXS, Need You Tonight
Paula Abdul, Straight Up

HUGHES THE BOSS: TEEN MOVIE SOUNDTRACK

OMD, If You Leave (Pretty in Pink)
Thompson Twins, If You Were Here
 (Sixteen Candles)
Simple Minds, Don't You (Forget About Me)
 (The Breakfast Club)
General Public, Taking the Day Off
 (Ferris Bueller's Day Off)
The Beatles, Twist and Shout
 (Ferris Bueller's Day Off)
Stephen Duffy, She Loves Me
 (Some Kind of Wonderful)
Oingo Boingo, Weird Science (Weird Science)
Van Halen, Pretty Woman (Weird Science)
Spandau Ballet, True (Sixteen Candles)
The Smiths, Please, Please, Please, Let Me Get
What I Want (Pretty in Pink)
Lick the Tins, Can't Help Falling in Love
 (Some Kind of Wonderful)

VIDEO KILLED THE RADIO STAR

Duran Duran, Rio
Michael Jackson, Thriller
Various, We Are the World
a-ha, Take on Me
Madonna, Material Girl
Run-D.M.C and Aerosmith, Walk This Way
Dire Straits, Money for Nothing
Beastie Boys, Sabotage
Cyndi Lauper, Girls Just Want to Have Fun
Tom Petty, Don't Come Around Here No More
Young MC, Bust a Move
Lionel Richie, Dancing on the Ceiling
Van Halen, Hot for Teacher
Culture Club, Karma Chameleon

RU GOING 2 THE DANCE???

Cake, The Distance
Usher, You Make Me Wanna...
Eve 6, Inside Out
Aaliyah, Are You That Somebody?
Smash Mouth, Walkin' on the Sun
Third Eye Blind, Semi-Charmed Life
Jamiroquai, Virtual Insanity
Backstreet Boys, I Want It That Way
Puff Daddy featuring R. Kelly, Satisfy You
Will Smith, Miami
Aerosmith, Don't Wanna Miss a Thing
The Notorious B.I.G., Mase & Puff Daddy,
   Mo Money Mo Problems
Everclear, Father of Mine
Ace of Base, The Sign
Fatboy Slim, Praise You
Pras featuring Ol' Dirty Bastard &
   Mya, Ghetto Supastar
Dave Matthews Band, Crash into Me

Y BREAKUP MIX

No Doubt, Don't Speak
White Town, Your Woman
Boyz II Men, Water Runs Dry
The Cardigans, Lovefool
Cat Power, The Greatest
Elliott Smith, Between the Bars
Wyclef Jean, Gone Till November
Ben Folds Five, Brick
Celine Dion, My Heart Will Go On
Justin Timberlake, Cry Me a River

GIRLS, GIRLS, GIRLS

Christina Aguilera, Genie in a Bottle
Spice Girls, Wannabe
Brandy & Monica, The Boy Is Mine
Gwen Stefani, Bubble Pop Electric
Lauryn Hill, Doo Wop (That Thing)
Liz Phair, Polyester Bride
Mariah Carey, Honey
Janet Jackson, Velvet Rope
Fiona Apple, Criminal
TLC, No Scrubs
Jewel, Who Will Save Your Soul
Madonna, Music
Britney Spears, (You Drive Me) Crazy
Sheryl Crow, All I Wanna Do
Alanis Morissette, Ironic

EARLY 2000s COOL KIDS

Belle & Sebastian, Dear Catastrophe Waitress
Thom Yorke, The Eraser
MGMT, Electric Feel
Hot Chip, Boy from School
Ladytron, Seventeen
CSS, Art Bitch
Radiohead, Down Is the New Up
The Shins, Kissing the Lipless
Death Cab for Cutie, President of What?
Lykke Li, Dance. Dance. Dance.

MADONNA WANNABE

X When I was growing up in the seventies and eighties, no one talked about corporations having "identities." A company might have an identity associated with it, like Ronald McDonald. But things have changed. These days, Ronald has all but disappeared from McDonald's marketing—because clowns are creepy, yes, but also because they're no longer needed. At some point, brands stopped using personalities and *became* personalities. Conversely, personalities have become brands. Back in the day, Oprah hosted a TV show. Today, she doesn't have time for that shit because she spends all day managing her brand (or "the Oprah").

For my generation—the first to become comfortable, for better or worse, with the idea that you could actually brand yourself—there's one figure who stands out as the living emblem of this transformation: Madonna.

For the benefit of any newly arrived extraterrestrials (OMG hi!), here's a quick review of what everyone on this planet already knows: Madonna, pop star, actress, director, children's book author, clothing designer, icon, and businesswoman, is the top-selling female recording artist in the United States. She has remained successful for thirty years through her ability to change musical styles, belief systems, hair colors, and accents, constantly finding new ways to make newly relevant her signature ingredients of sex, spirituality, co-opted subculture, good songwriting, and of-the-moment collaborators. I have loved her a lot for a long time, though never so much as when I was in college and reading the kind of French theory that showed me how to elevate that love into something intellectually defensible.

More than that, though, she has been a near-infallible guide to reimagining the self as brand. From very early on, Madonna approached her public persona as consumer commodity—that is, something that offers not only a straightforward value proposition ("these are good songs that gay men /cougars / bar mitzvah guests will dance to") but also the promise of a relationship that delivers across many touchpoints not just a service or product but a feeling about yourself and your life ("this is someone who recognizes you for who you are and makes you feel good about yourself"). And as her brand grew, it became clear that "pop singer" was no longer enough to contain or define what Madonna was becoming, and not only because she was actively expanding her résumé by acting in films and launching her own entertainment company.

While there were many versions of Madonna over the years—pseudo-Latina Catholic school renegade, hennaed electronica yogi, classic screen diva–inspired gay icon, kabbalistic space cowgirl—these were all images and ideas being masterminded by someone, the Real Madonna, the branding-expert Madonna, from behind an Oz-like curtain. That Madonna, a person we've never seen and never can, has a remarkable talent for reading the culture, distilling it, and creating something that's just the right mix of catchy and provocative. More than that, though, she has that hard-to-capture ability to connect with her consumer and imbue that connection, however mediated and massified, with a sense of meaning and emotion. Her public persona continues to fascinate us.

For me, that first and defining moment was the song "Express Yourself," a girl-power anthem whose famous video paid homage to Fritz Lang's *Metropolis*. If you'd asked why I loved it, I couldn't have told you—that is, I would have given an answer that employed a lot of lingo from my women's studies and critical theory classes, but I wouldn't have been telling the truth. The truth was that I found the song beautiful, and the lyrics, banal as they were, spoke to me: "Don't go for second best, baby / put your love to the test / you know you know you've got to." Hackneyed though the sentiment was, it exhorted me to do something that I, and lots of women I knew, couldn't do: Ask for what we wanted, expect more, demand authenticity from ourselves and from our partners. Hell, I still can't do that, but I want to. Which may be why my pulse still quickens to the opening bars of that song.

Madonna's real genius is what marketing experts have always known: Understand your product, know what it does best and for whom. She understands what a great pop song does: It doesn't invent new sensations but rather identifies existing ones and gives us a new outlet through which to express and share them.

MARKETING 101 WITH MADONNA

Here are some of the specific things Madonna the brand-master taught us.

1 Your product doesn't have to be entirely original

This is something Steve Jobs also made reference to: Don't bother inventing the newest, coolest thing. Find the person doing it and hire them—or just steal their idea. Usually, the people on the bleeding edge of innovation aren't the ones who reap its final rewards. From adopting the practice of voguing from the gay dance scene to hiring prominent producers of drum-and-bass and electronica, Madonna has always had a knack for seeking out those who are pushing musical boundaries and using them to expand her horizons—while gently pushing those elements closer to mainstream acceptance.

2 Your product has to be consistent in some way

This seems like a weird thing to say about Madonna, but it's actually true. In Madonna's case, she has recognized that her brand IS about change; rather than become known for one thing, she is known for never sticking to one thing. That's her brand promise, and she makes good on it by reinventing herself.

3 You should care about quality

Whether you're a fan or not, it's pretty apparent that Madonna works hard to produce solid, relevant dance music. Madonna respects her audience and her competition enough to know she still has to deliver quality albums and singles.

4 Pay attention to what's going on around you

Adapt. The world changes quickly these days, and staying current involves a delicate process of choosing which current trends and elements will work with your brand and adapting them to be relevant to your persona and product. No matter how much it might embarrass your daughter.

5 Don't be all things to all people

Being distinctive and memorable means, by definition, being disliked by some. Being acceptable or inoffensive to everyone is death to a brand; inspiring loyalties and strong opinions (even if some are negative) equals success. And a buttload of cash.

MADONNA AND JUSTIFYING GEN Y'S LOVE

Y

Madonna and I have one thing in common: Nonni. It's my middle name, one that I rarely reveal because it basically means Leonora "Grandmother" Epstein, but I digress. Nonni also happens to be Madonna's childhood nickname; her family called her this to distinguish her from her mother, also named Madonna.

It is not easy to find something you have in common with the world's biggest pop star. Even if you both adore the color orange and have a thing for younger men, Madonna has a way of rendering any counterpoint null because, well, is she even a real person?

With Madonna, there's no "Stars! They're just like us!" because she's not even a star. More like fabric of the universe.

At least, this is how Gen Y comprehends Madonna. While Gen X may have witnessed the birth and growth of the pop icon, we came into a world where she already existed, and as a result, Madonna's been an implicit aspect of our pop-culture curriculum. So it's almost an irrelevant question to ask a Millennial if she listens to Madonna, because: *duh*. For us, she's always been an icon and a presence, one so revered that we're inevitably distanced from it.

Which is why, even when I realize that Madonna and I share this one extremely personal, unique, and cool thing—Nonni—I feel nothing. Why? Because one does not *relate* to Madonna. Adores and respects, perhaps. But in your relationship with Madonna, she *gives* experiences and revelations but never really participates.

For Gen Y, the experiences Madonna bequeathed upon us existed in two separate domains.

First, there was Madonna 1.0, an original, mythic vintage relic characterized by all her most classic hits of the eighties like "Vogue," "Lucky Star," "Like a Virgin," and a wardrobe containing pointy b ras, rosaries, fingerless lace gloves—the stuff that would become costume templates for eighties nights and Halloweens. While she gave us fabulous memories, these came with larger cultural connotations already attached. This was the Madonna who opened our eyes to her importance and made us realize that not knowing the lyrics to the songs in the Madonna canon was unacceptable. Knowing how to Vogue-dance, seeing Madonna roll on a floor in a wedding dress, singing "Borderline" at karaoke—these are true American rites of passage.

And then there was Madonna 2.0, which was pretty much everything after that. This was the point at which Madonna would reinvent herself with new identities faster than we could—there was the kabbalah-mystic-electronica witch of "Frozen," the pop-cowgirl of "Music," the seventies disco-dancing diva of "Hung Up," and then, well, it starts to become a blur. From there, Madonna became something like a constantly changing background. And kind of like a slideshow screen saver, you could choose to sit and enjoy it for a bit, or turn it off and move on to other things.

The only time these two entities would meet would be at the 2003 MTV Video Music Awards, when Britney Spears and Madonna kissed on live TV. Depending on what generation you're in, this was either the best thing ever or a sign of the apocalypse.

Madonna 2.0 would distance us from 1.0, thanks in part to a technology boom that would catalyze a cultural saturation point for a lot of things. As Madonna and the Internet were a match made in heaven, the Madonna of our formative Gen Y years would become so mass, you'd have a hard time holding on to anything. You could recognize all her latest videos but not remember when you contributed to that twenty-four million and rising hit count. You could know she was on tour but not know how you heard that. Or you could have her latest album in your iTunes library but not recall the moment you illegally downloaded it.

The thing is, while we can't deny Madonna's existence and makeup of the background of our world, we also can't lay claim to the era in which she was most significant—the one where Madge was upsetting the Pope and pissing off parents for putting raw, unapologetic sex in the open.

For Gen Yers who matured in an age when Marilyn Manson was being blamed for school shootings and access to porn became easier than checking out a library book, Madonna couldn't be the divisive figure and controversial icon for us that she was for Gen X. Age aside, she didn't stand a chance of becoming a face of our generation.

Instead, we wound up with Lady Gaga.

OVERLAP ACTS

overlap acts, *noun, pl.*: bands and artists that have managed (whether for better or worse) to cultivate both X and Y identities over a period of time.

There is little rhyme or reason to musical overlaps; they achieve their status through varied paths, and the success of gaining such status isn't necessarily a reflection of critical success. But artists who manage to maintain a career spanning several decades enter a special intergenerational X/Y discourse—one that either pits us against one another or highlights our appreciation of one another.
  To wit:

BONO

X

Earnest, political, activist front man
with awful hair, known for belting out
remarkably well-crafted pop songs with
arrestingly angsty soul.

Y

Douche. With weird sunglasses.

LIZ PHAIR

X

Y

Following her release of *Exile in Guyville* in '93, Phair becomes the veritable queen of lo-fi indie girl rockers, known in her songs for her blunt and raw treatment of relationships, until . . .

Phair releases a self-titled album in 2003 featuring a pop-y, mainstream sound with accompanying album art that could have just as easily been a bad *GQ* spread.

MADONNA

X

Y

A legend-in-the-making with songs engineered to be hits and a controversial sexual agenda to keep it going . . .

. . . and going, and going. Still a pop star at fifty. NBD.

BEASTIE BOYS

X

Y

First white rappers to earn respect thanks to inventive samples and superb lyrical mastery; they build a hipster empire of well-received hip-hop recordings (*Licensed to Ill, Paul's Boutique, Check Your Head*), a street fashion brand (X-Large), a recording label (Grand Royal), and even a magazine.

1998 sees the *Hello Nasty* era—a Y2K lead-up fueled by old-school beats with a futuristic veneer. One that you could dance pretty hard to.

JANET JACKSON

X

Y

Adorable kid sister of Michael et al. who first gains fame as a TV actress (*Diff'rent Strokes*); she then changes her image in 1986 with the release of the attitude-heavy album *Control*, containing the now-famous phrase "It's Janet— Miss Jackson if you're nasty."

Janet goes emotionally bare in *The Velvet Rope* (1997), an album that gives her a more soulful sound and deeper character.

STING

X

Y

Front man for Brit rock/new wave/reggae- and punk-influenced band the Police through the mid-eighties, reborn as a jazz-inflected singer-songwriter and overcelebrated practitioner of tantric sex.

Writer/singer of songs for such cinematic masterpieces as *Kate & Leopold* and *The Emperor's New Groove*.

RADIOHEAD

X

Y

Sorrowful, self-loathing and/or dark lyrics and catchy melodies on songs like "Creep" and "High and Dry" in the early to mid-nineties draw the attention of shoegazers and Pixies fans, then gain more traction with later releases (*OK Computer, Kid A*).

By the time Radiohead releases their pay-what-you-want album *In Rainbows* in 2007, they've already solidified their spot as the foundation to any hipster's musical library.

FIRST CONCERT: NOT WITH A WHAM! BUT A WHIMPER

Today at enormous arena rock shows, 90 percent of the attendees are strangely content to view a "live" performance on LED screens posted throughout impossibly large venues.

My first concert was not like that.

It was Wham!—who, though already a huge sensation, were for some reason booked in the Beacon Theatre, a small venue across the street from my home on the Upper West Side of Manhattan.

While not exactly an early adopter of Wham!'s oeuvre (I was not, for instance, familiar with their first album, featuring the intriguingly named "Wham Rap"), I had certainly been thoroughly swept up in the craze surrounding the sunny pop duo, and I was totally enamored of front man George Michael. I remember looking at pictures of his face and thinking to myself that it was the embodiment of perfection, staring at his outrageously white teeth and gravity-eschewing head-soufflé of airily frosted and feathered hair and finding every single thing about him beautiful.

Anyway. It was February 14, 1985, and my best friend, Allegra, had managed to talk her parents into buying us tickets. Even better, all respective guardians had given their permission for us to attend the show sans chaperone—a decision we mistakenly attributed to their amazing trust in us despite our tender age (thirteen); the real reason certainly had more to do with the fact that not one of the four adults in question could be expected voluntarily to subject his or her eardrums to the strains of "Wake Me Up Before You Go-Go" and other such (perceived) inanities.

We were in the eighth row—great seats with a pretty unobstructed view of the performers. But even with so much proximity, they felt no closer to me than if I'd been watching them on MTV. Back then, famous people just weren't people to me. They weren't made of flesh. They didn't breathe air or get colds or go to the bathroom or feel things.

But they could sing. The music was great. George Michael's vocal prowess was something even my classical musician parents had to concede; even buried under so much mid-eighties frippery, his croon was hypnotic. The highlight of the evening was "Careless Whisper," the beautiful and heartbreaking ballad that seemed like the emotional counterpart to "Wake Me Up"—the tragic potential consequences of *not* waking your partner up before you go-go, I assumed. The lights were dimmed, the lighters were lit and held aloft—a gesture that has since become acceptable only as a show of irony—and the crowd became one silent but teeming entity of enchantment, swaying like grasses in the breeze of that plaintive sax solo.

And then, as the song wound down, the screaming resumed. The audience was almost entirely composed of girls between the ages of thirteen and seventeen, and as a result the noise from the crowd remained at a constant and unnervingly high pitch and decibel level. I remember experiencing, for the first time, that uncomfortable buzzing that is your eardrums' way of telling you that a sonic assault is verging on the unacceptable and threatening to incur permanent damage—not the music, in this case, but the primal and unending sounds issuing from the girls to my left and to my right.

Afterward, we were physically exhausted but so revved—by the crowd, the music, the ringing in our ears, the aftermath of all that expectation, and the first-timeness of it all—that we somehow knew we'd never get to sleep that night. My father, in an act of supreme awesomeness, told us we could play hooky the next day. It was, all in all, a perfect evening.

Sometime later, I read an article detailing some of the goings-on at certain Wham! shows, and one thing stood out to me: Apparently, the boys were known for shoving shuttlecocks down their shorts and then batting them out into the audience (presumably with badminton rackets, though I don't actually remember). At thirteen, and a young thirteen at that, I was appalled and relieved that I hadn't had to contend with such a performance. It struck me as disgusting and unsanitary and vaguely frightening. It did not seem to be in keeping with the image of them I held to—that of animated Ken dolls with frozen smiles and nothing but smooth plastic down the fronts (and backs) of their pants—or for that matter, the image they themselves appeared to promote as adorable but nonsexual confections whose lyrics hinged on the rhyming of "go-go" and "yo-yo." Something about this information broke the fourth wall of my desire. It let in too much of something too real. And while nothing could ever destroy the sanctity of that concert, it did forever alter my feelings about George Michael as a love object. Which, I suspect, he's not too broken up over.

FIRST CONCERT:
THE ONE WITH THE JESUS LIZARD

 You Anne, Molly, and Lisa had gone to the Crossgates Mall in Albany to see Aqua, and I had not been invited. This was not OK.

The fact that Molly's mom was the type of mom who would willingly drive three hyper teenage girls one hour to go see a Danish-Norwegian dance-pop band whose only known song to most of mankind ("Barbie Girl") would later be named "The Worst Song of the Nineties" by *Rolling Stone*, was just, like, not fair.

In school on Monday, the trio bounced around the halls shrieking the hiccup-like, ditzerrific lyrics, eliciting the raunchy baritone notes from the seventh-grade boys who lowered their voices as best they could to sing, "Come on, Barbie, let's go party," to which the girls responded with that squeaky and impossibly high-pitched "ah, ah, ah yeah!"

What was going *on*? These were my *best friends*. And though I now have to assume that this was their first concert (although I'm not sure how seeing a one-hit Euro-pop band *in a mall, in the daytime* counts), they had suddenly been put in a class of cooler adolescence—people who went to see live music because their parents let them.

"They touched my hand, they touched my HAND!!!" Anne shrieked repeatedly that day. She really wanted to make sure everyone knew this.

What was I going to do? I needed to lose my concert virginity. Doing this in western Massachusetts with parents who definitely would not drive you an hour to *any* place—even if you really tried to explain to them how your life depended on it—would be difficult.

But I did have my totally cool older sister who lived in Hollywood, and at twelve years old, I had recently earned the privilege of making what would become regular solo trips out to Los Angeles for vacation visits. These trips would end up saving me during my teenage years and also give me a taste for everything that wasn't in *Teen People*, *YM*, or the Crossgates Mall, for that matter.

On this trip out to the West Coast, I wanted to go to a concert, I told Eve. It was very important that this be accomplished, I stressed, so Eve took out a newspaper to look at what was on that week. There weren't many options considering the show had to be all ages, but the Jesus Lizard was playing at the Roxy. I didn't know who these pious reptilians were, but it didn't matter.

Struggling to stay awake the night of, I fished through the piles of Betsey Johnson dresses, ripped jeans, and boyish button-ups on the floor of Eve's studio apartment; almost equally important as attending a rock show was the outfit you wore to it. Finally I found the perfect thing: a white T-shirt with baby blue edging and a shiny, glitter-patterned iron-on reading "KISS." As you can probably guess, I had no clue this was the logo of the heavy metal band. I just thought it was, like, *kiss*, you know? So cute.

With that, I wore some baggy blue corduroys with platform sneakers and clipped my straightened hair back with colorful clips on both sides.

This was going to be so cool.

When we entered the Roxy, my excitement was quickly replaced by fear. I had to have been the youngest person there and was pretty sure I wasn't supposed to be there and we were going to get kicked out and maybe go to jail. As we waited in the semidarkness for the show to begin, I tried my best to seem chill, but behind us a girl with a cropped top and a belly-button ring was furiously making out with a guy, and I was pretty sure they were just going to have sex right there.

But nothing could prepare me for the moment when a sweaty and shirtless David Yow took the stage and began to act like what I can only describe as a really angry monster vomiting into a microphone. He whipped himself around while a violently loud, growling bass shook through my body, and behind him, Animal the Muppet beat up his drum kit.

The sound was unhinging. But it was mainly the vocals that made me feel like a million horror movies all at once. To give you a better idea, *Entertainment Weekly*'s 1994 review of the group's live album, *Show*, describes how "Yow alternately squeals like a stuck pig and hollers like a caveman with a throat full of phlegm," and the magazine's later review of *Shot* in '96 acknowledges the band's lack of restraint: "Yow spat out demented lyrics as the band lurched along in fits and starts like drunks trying to play the Stooges' songbook."

It goes without saying that hearing all this was terrifying.

Once you have experienced the Jesus Lizard, they are hard to forget. If you have never heard of this noise-rock band, all you really need to know is that the Jesus Lizard live is what your parents *think* a rock show is like, except it *is actually what your parents think a rock show is like*. It is bad-influence musicians playing loud music you really don't get, in an atmosphere charged with pent-up anger, and a front man who might trample you, disrobe, dismember stuffed animals, or even lick you, as I read Yow was prone to doing. (If this happened, I have blocked it out.)

My sister taking me to see them for my first rock show was either brilliant or the world's worst idea.

Although I'm thinking it's neither, because I'm pretty sure when I got home I told everyone the concert I'd seen was Aqua.

BEATS THE ALTERNATIVE

The first time I heard "Smells Like Teen Spirit," I was in the Williams College radio station with my friend listening to records. They put on *Nevermind*, and we proceeded to lose our minds over how "important" it was, noting that it was a watershed single, the sort of crossover that would change everything forever, for better and worse. What we didn't know was that it was already happening: "Smells Like Teen Sprit" was by then number six on *Billboard*.

I think it's pretty much agreed that Nirvana's *Nevermind* was the record that transformed alternative music from a legitimate subculture into a subgenre of mainstream popular music. And as such, it's ironically representative of both the apotheosis of that genre and its demise—its moment of greatest triumph, and the beginning of its undoing. (It's tough not to read Kurt Cobain's suicide as the ultimate acknowledgment of this, but let's hope he had better reasons.) Why demise and undoing? Because the minute that sound entered the mainstream, it began its inevitable journey toward becoming something wretched and diluted; it began to turn into things like Creed and Nickelback. Yet while Nirvana was inextricably linked to this devolution, you can't really blame them for it.

If you have to blame someone, you should probably blame me. Well, not me, per se, but people like me. Because it was people like me who unwittingly were the bridge from obscurity to mainstream acceptance, positioned as we were at the crossroads.

I was a college radio DJ groupie. Admitting this is hard, for the obvious reason that it makes me pretty lame. Music was a big part of my youth and my college experience, but I was not an early adopter—and back in those days, loving indie rock was all about being an early adopter. I didn't have a *Sub Pop* singles subscription or my own radio show on the college station. I didn't salivate at the prospect of a Lou Barlow sighting or drive all night just to catch a glimpse of Guy Picciotto. I didn't have an encyclopedic knowledge of Pixies lore or riot grrrl discographies. I liked all that stuff, but I left the digging and discovery to my friends, and I was aware that for our Gen X music culture that meant I was less cool. The whole point of being a "music person" was to be a discoverer and catalog of the obscure and the undiscovered; to leave that to others and simply breeze through on their coattails made me a much less cool sort of person, a co-opter of someone else's expertise, a collector of other people's hard-won knowledge, a poser. Which is precisely why Nirvana was so incredibly important for me.

There was something about that Nirvana album that made it feel like it belonged to you. It didn't matter if you were the first person to hear it or the last; it became just as much yours as it was anyone else's. Which, of course, is something all good music does: It resists mediation and compartmentalization; it transcends. Whereas other bands I listened to were always a degree or two removed from me, somehow the borrowed property of cooler people who'd discovered them first; Nirvana was mine. It was accessible in the best possible sense of the word in that it was great songwriting and great playing produced slickly enough to sound equally good to people who loved pop, metal, or punk rock.

The problem is, of course, that for people like Kurt Cobain, there's some crucial utility in being inaccessible: It's a barrier that keeps out the wrong types of fans. Once Nirvana crossed over, once the music stopped being the property of a small and self-selected group of incredibly like-minded people, it opened the door to any number of undesirables. For Cobain, these included sexist assholes, abortion opponents, racists, and homophobes. By definition, you don't get to have the number-one album in the country without having a few homophobic fans. But opening that door let people like me in, too, and we're not an altogether terrible sort. And while it's occasionally surprising to hear "In Bloom" on the mainstream classic rock station, it still beats the alternative scenario in which Nirvana disappears into obscurity and is remembered by only the aging early adopters cool enough to recognize its genius.

GROWING UP Y: THE SPICE GIRLS AND GIRL POWER

 When I taped over the only copy of my bat mitzvah video to record a Spice Girls lip sync with my best friends, I was fully aware of the disastrous consequences that would inevitably ensue.

What can I say? There was no blank tape, and "Wannabe" was cued up and ready to go. I channeled my inner badass Scary Spice and made a choice.

I knew the day would come when my mother would pop in that bat mitzvah video and find that halfway through my wobbly Torah portion, she'd see—cut!—five imposter Spice Girls singing into hairbrushes. That I'd be in big trouble was a given. But the Spice Girls understood that defying your mother was part of being a woman. That's why there was track number six, "Mama," on their debut album, which was all about maternal redemption: *Mama I love you / Mama I care / You're my friend.*

"Spicemania"—the term that came to describe the worldwide frenzy over what is still the number-one best-selling girl group—is no exaggeration. For girls coming of age in the late nineties, Victoria, Mel C, Mel B, Emma, and Geri were leaders of a "girl power" revolution we clung to, no matter how manufactured it was. And despite the fact that the British-born bunch was actually a strong representation of Gen Xers (with birth years ranging 1972–1976), the audience they catered to was distinctly Gen Y.

For those of us who spent 1996–1998 flaunting peace signs and decorating notebooks with "girl power" written in bubble letters, we're now well aware that the Spice Girls were a product of some very successful and manipulative marketing. But that doesn't undo the authenticity of our relationships to those girls, the music, and the culture they brought with them.

The Spice Girls' message was clear: Ladies, here is your permission to kick butt. Plus, you can be smart *and* pretty while doing it. This came at a time when girlhood wasn't particularly colorful. When the group's first album, *Spice*, reached the U.S. in 1997, *Reviving Ophelia*, the psychological examination of the dark world of adolescent girls, was in its third year on the *New York Times* best-seller list. Female teens were a troubled bunch, producing a growing collection of terrifying statistics about depression, eating disorders, confidence, and sex—and a lot of it had to do with male objectification.

When it came to girl power, the band was unabashedly unapologetic about their no-boys-allowed attitude. Interviewers (especially the male ones) who questioned the singers about men were often met with a loud chorus of dissent, and the girls had a knack for putting inquiring minds in their place. During one American radio interview during which the deejay asked about "picking up guys," Scary Spice started a smackdown, shouting:

> **SCARY SPICE**: Excuse me! This is about *girl power*; this isn't about picking up *guys* . . . we don't need men to control our lives. We control our lives anyway.
>
> **DEEJAY:** That's what I'm saying. Pick up some American men you can control!
>
> **SCARY:** No . . . you haven't got it!
>
> **GINGER SPICE (in an ooh-burn manner)**: Do you think you need controlling, then? Speaking on behalf of the American men? Because we'll happily come down there to Seattle and educate you.

This side of girl power—sticking with your girlfriends and standing up to boys—was something we needed; for many of us, this would be our first introduction to feminism. And while this school of feminism might have had a shiny, packaged veneer and come with some ethos we may now find questionable, it was clear about female empowerment and positivity.

Of course, those who loved the Spice Girls weren't necessarily immune to the darkness of nineties teenagedom. But for many of us, the pop group gave us a reprieve from it all and provided a space for identity experimentation.

Just as we were getting boobs, the Spice Girls gave us a range of female identities to try on. Sporty Spice was a ripped, stylish athlete; Baby remember when i made that list of heavy metal musicians?

 no! who was on it

it had, like, all the things i needed for a basic education in rock and shit

like deaf leopard

 DEF LEPPARD

right i know. anyhow, i lost the list.

so who should i know? basically...what are the songs people do at karaoke and radio songs? i feel like i can sing along to these things but i don't know who sings them.

 um ok. well probably there are a few van halen songs like that

"jump"

"panama" etc

you know who they are right?

yes

 and journey is always v popular. and obviously bon jovi

is bon jovi really good?

 uh

YES.

38

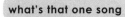

 i mean, kind of.

what's that one song

 "livin' on a prayer"? "wanted dead or alive"?

ugh i dunno. there's too much. i'm overwhelmed. i feel like such an idiot.

 noooo.

i feel like an idiot because i don't know this stuff and i just pretend to know. and then i just google stuff really fast

 haha. that's very Gen X. but don't people see you doing it?

no because i am magic.

i mean all i know about '80s music is whatever is on what new mix cd you give me for my car. someone recently asked me to help with a list of essential '80s songs, and i was like...ummm christopher cross? which i then learned was not a cool response. but you made me listen to him. and so now i am confused.

 haha. yeah. that's not really cool at all

but you listen to christopher cross!

 i know. but it's more in the "guilty pleasure" category. like i wouldn't brag about that.

jeez. ok. well you need to tell me these things from now on when you give me a new mix. or at least categorize the mixes into "songs that make you cooler" and "songs you should not tell people about."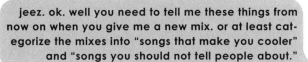

was a pig-tailed angel who capitalized on cuteness; Scary was a wild animal; Posh was a collected adult with high-fashion sense; and Ginger was the loud-mouthed sexy one.

Some of my friends immediately adopted and stuck with a single Spice Girl personality. As for me, my favorites changed frequently. I loved Scary's style and her ferocious confidence. And while I thought I was really a Ginger at heart, I took comfort in embodying Baby's safe immaturity on days I felt guilty about and scared of my growing sexual identity. That these characters are stereotypes is of course obvious now, but back then they gave us a fun selection of fashion styles and attitudes to start with.

In conversations with Gen X, it's been hard to get all these points across because they're able to see what I can't deny to be the truth: that the Spice Girls are *not actually good.* Spice Girls fans don't throw on "Spice Up Your Life" in a flight of ironic fancy the way people do with Journey or Depeche Mode. We will never again be caught dead wearing platform sneakers or latex minidresses.

If Gen X considered the Spice Girls to be just another musical phenomenon destined for obsolescence in a couple of years, they were also right about that. The quintet produced only three albums. The first two came in consecutive years—*Spice* in 1996, *Spiceworld* in 1997—and tore up the charts. But by the release of their unintentionally ironically named third album, *Forever,* in 2000, their following had waned considerably; the record performed poorly, and Geri Halliwell had already departed the band two years prior.

So, in the end, Spicemania might have been fleeting, but its effects stayed with us. And if Gen Xers can't get that, then there's only one thing to say: *Who do you think you are?*

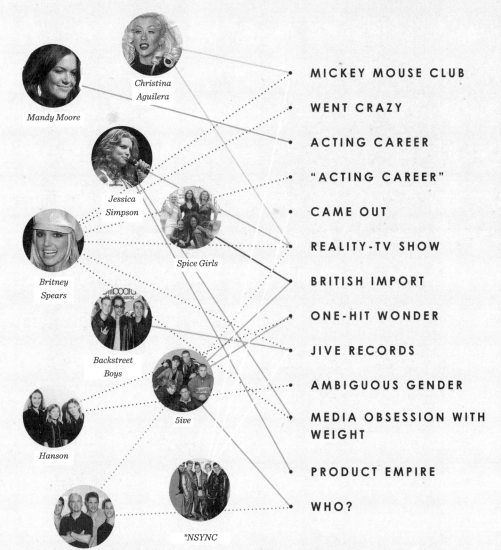

A BASIC GUIDE TO BOY BANDS AND BUBBLEGUM POP

Christina Aguilera

Mandy Moore

Jessica Simpson

Spice Girls

Britney Spears

Backstreet Boys

Hanson

5ive

*NSYNC

98 Degrees

MICKEY MOUSE CLUB

WENT CRAZY

ACTING CAREER

"ACTING CAREER"

CAME OUT

REALITY-TV SHOW

BRITISH IMPORT

ONE-HIT WONDER

JIVE RECORDS

AMBIGUOUS GENDER

MEDIA OBSESSION WITH WEIGHT

PRODUCT EMPIRE

WHO?

GRUNGE

DELIA*S

VALLEY GIRLS

URBAN
OUTFITTERS

HARD
CANDY

GUNNE
SAX

BODY
GLITTER

MARC JACOBS

BENETTON

BETSEY
JOHNSON

JELLY SANDALS

PLATFORM
SNEAKERS

SWATCH

CHAPTER 2

FASHION

———

Style Icon Wall of Fame

On the walls and timelines that are the default metaphors for our lives, there are some figures who deserve extra-pretty frames. Here are the ladies, real and fictional, who shaped our personal style.

2

4

1

3

5

1980   **1985**   **1990**

Y

1. Claire Danes
2. Drew Barrymore
3. Jennifer Lopez
4. Nicole Richie
5. Gwen Stefani
6. Mary-Kate and
   Ashley Olsen
7. Lindsay Lohan
8. Beyoncé

2

1

3

7

6

8

X
1. Molly Ringwald
2. Naomi Campbell
3. Kim Gordon
4. Courtney Love
5. Lisa Bonet
6. Winona Ryder
7. Sofia Coppola
8. Kate Moss

1995   **2000**   **2005**   **2010**

5

7

8

4

6

X INTRO

FASHION POLICE

I attended a private prep school on the Upper East Side of Manhattan in the eighties. And while there were no uniforms, there may as well have been: tapered Levi's or Guess jeans, Benetton rugby shirts, and Tretorns for the girls; Polo shirts and Levi's for the boys. There were better, more interesting forms of fashion to be found—goths, art-school wannabes, metalheads, hippies—but this unofficial eighties prepster-meets-Eurotrash uniform prevailed. And while it wasn't very good fashion, it *was* fashion in the sense that it was a language, a way of telling the world something about yourself— in this case, *I belong* or, at least, *I want to.*

For Gen X, fashion is the front lines of identity, the cover by which we fully expect our books to be judged. Back then, you could tell just by looking at someone what music they liked, what their politics were, what part of town they were from. You could make a reasonable guess as to which extra-curriculars they pursued and whom they hung out with. Today, the world has changed: I've met many a twentysomething whose outward image is only just that—not a signaling of what lies beneath but a surface donned to communicate a passing whim, a well-developed sense of irony, or, one can only assume, incipient insanity. If I see a Gen Xer wearing a Def Leppard shirt, I confidently anticipate reminiscing with him about the days when drummer Rick Allen had two arms. When I see a Gen Yer wearing one, I assume that they think *Rock of Ages* is a movie starring Tom Cruise that came out in 2012. Now, you're thinking, that's unfair—Def Leppard is Gen X stuff, so of course you'd expect a Gen Xer to get the reference. But it holds true no matter which era is being referenced—Gen Xers wear clothing that gestures toward eras past, from hippie garb to classic rock tees. But when we wear it, we're consciously paying tribute to those eras and identifying ourselves through them. We trust in the authenticity of objects and their ability to convey meaning across time and space. (See also: vinyl, *Star Wars* action figures, collections of every sort.) Gen Yers, in a word, don't.

You might expect me to hate this particular quality in my juniors— their penchant for treating fashion as something infinitely disposable and pretty meaningless—but I don't. Oh, sure, I have my moments of wanting to bludgeon the odd youngster for blithely and ignorantly appropriating the hallowed sartorial signifiers of my (or someone else's) youth—Doc Martens, Swatches, combat boots, flannel shirts, peace signs, polyester, fifties secretary garb, Top-Siders, and fanny packs all dizzyingly commingle in their closets like ingredients in an ill-seasoned melting pot—but in truth, they've got a point. It's like they're telling us they won't play our reindeer games, the ones where we presort ourselves into groups before even saying hi, scanning the room for "our people," gravitating toward the chick in the Dinosaur Jr. T-shirt, and silently judging the dude with the puka beads.

Don't they have a point? The truth is, I can relate. At the end of high school, after having toiled unsuccessfully for many years to fit in, I took a sharp left turn: A summer visit to Tokyo (where my mother lived) introduced me to the street stalls of Shibuya and Harajuku and the racks of the Ginza, and I returned a new sort of person in clashing-hued striped shirts, chartreuse terrycloth baby-doll dresses, bright green overalls, Raggedy Ann pajama bottoms, billowy red bloomers with white polka dots, battered old hiking boots paired with eensy miniskirts and iridescent metallic tights, blood-red lipstick, and platinum-blonde hair. It was a riotous explosion of color and form, but one without much specific meaning: It wasn't exactly punk, it wasn't entirely hippie, it wasn't exactly pop queen. If anything, it was the first time in my life that it occurred to me that fashion could be a way to stand out, rather than blend in, and I was saying that: I'm no longer trying to fit in, to speak your language. Which isn't all that different from what I see the members of Gen Y doing: They reject the enslavement to "meaning" conveyed by one or another article of clothing, choosing instead to inhabit a frivolously postmodern state of playfulness about the whole thing.

In the end, I think both generations' stances are necessary for true fashion smartness. When I think of great dressers, they have a knack for uniting the two: They understand the myriad of references at their disposal and wield them deftly when they choose, but they also get that fashion is much more and much less than all of that and something to be taken way less seriously. And that's definitely a good thing. Because without a sense of humor and an awareness of its own meaninglessness, fashion is just a bunch of badly dressed high school kids making you feel bad about yourself.

Y INTRO

EVERYTHING OLD IS NEW AGAIN

Like many female best friends, Holly Block and I hated each other. Or at least, we were fiercely competitive, usually over who could sing *The Little Mermaid* soundtrack with the most intensity (me, obviously) and who could do a one-handed cartwheel better (I'll finally concede defeat twenty years later).

But for the most part, our relationship revolved around another woman: *Saved by the Bell*'s Kelly Kapowski. Holly and I worshipped Bayside High's most popular pupil—as portrayed by a bubby Tiffani Amber Thiessen—and we engaged in a constant war over who could best embody Kelly by trying to top each other's "Kelly outfits."

Pure nineties, Kelly's wardrobe consisted of colorful miniskirts, denim jackets, high-rise tapered jeans, off-the-shoulder tops, and oversized tees covered with garish neon graphics. You could tap into Kelly's fashion sense with relative ease by concentrating on the details: side-ponies, knotted T-shirt hems secured with velvet scrunchies or those plastic circles you'd weave the material through, DIY sweatshirts decorated with pearl puffy paints. Or at school, you could just carry around a binder like Kelly and the rest of the backpackless Baysiders. (Never mind that in first grade there's no real need to be toting around a Trapper Keeper all day.)

The real sartorial coups, however, were getting your parents to buy you a pair of pink Keds or a polka-dotted spandex top. I'll forever rue the day Holly Block showed up to school wearing a matching floral denim miniskirt and jean jacket. It was the perfect Kelly outfit that could only be topped by a tropical bikini with high-cut briefs; at seven years old, there was no way.

As far as female Gen Y style icons go, Kelly Kapowski has emerged as something of a surprising leader. You'd think that Lisa Turtle—with her color-block blazers, crazy hat collection, and coordinated outfits so detailed they practically required assembly instructions—would have had a better shot at maintaining a top-tier foothold. Lisa Turtle will, of course, forever have a beloved spot in our catalog of the past, but it was Kelly who became an artifact of Gen Y Americana, perhaps because her predictability and suburban banality made her an easy generalization to hold on to.

But there's also another thing: Gen Y gets off on reviving unlikely trends, and we support an ever-growing fascination with observing the reincarnations of self-referential fashion. Up until a few years ago, we would have put Kelly in the "what not to wear" pages, but as our fondness for irony grew, all of a sudden you began seeing signs of her—a neon crop top here, a pastel sundress there—along with some of her other TV contemporaries, like the sunflower-hatted Blossom Russo.

Of course, American Apparel has been the champion of hipster invention, furnishing us for years now with reproductions of the past such as leggings, stonewashed denim, fanny packs, or my personal favorite, short-shorts for men. In looking at Gen Y's fashion trajectory, you almost have to discount AA because the company's made it its business to put us in metallic leotards and sweatbands by force. Irony is what you expect at American Apparel; walk into any given outpost and you'll undoubtedly experience a moment of feeling like you're perusing wares in a costume shop. It's hard to take them seriously.

It's when you begin seeing signs of the past—on your friends and at retailers so obviously guided by trend forecasting—that you know a revival is really back. I remember walking into Topshop in the summer of 2010 and being overwhelmed with a wave of printed denim, acid washes, shapeless floral dresses, and miniature backpacks. Everything I'd ever worn before the age of ten was there, just slightly modernized for today's hipster. It was like looking at the aftermath of a three-way between *Clarissa Explains It All*, Elaine Benes, and Terry Richardson. It was both highly disturbing and fantastic.

While we've happily adopted reruns with Gen X roots (grunge, *Annie Hall* style, and eighties dancewear, to name a few), we're now beginning to look to our own pasts, and there's tons of material there to pull from, even if we maintain mixed feelings about some of it. Gen Y did a great job of supporting distinctive style movements—chances are you participated in several of them and changed your identity accordingly. We had goths, skaters, bohemians, tracksuit princesses, Abercrombie prepsters, ghetto-fabulous girls, emos, Harajuku girls, MySpace hipsters, ravers, granola guys, *Clueless* chicks, and so many more.

EVERYTHING OLD IS NEW AGAIN

X	Y
MY SO-CALLED LIFE POST-GRUNGE	MARY-KATE OLSEN HOBO-CHIC
NICE GIRLS OF 1991: Kelly Kapowski, Blossom Russo, Elaine Benes, Clarissa Darling	TOPSHOP 2010
CLUELESS SCHOOLGIRLS	*GOSSIP GIRLS*
HAMMER STYLE	HIGH-FASHION HAREM PANTS
FRESH PRINCE OF BEL-AIR	KOOK HIPSTERS WITH NEON HATS AND PARKAS

We're also defined by some of the saddest moments in fashion history, which no amount of Eternal Sunshining will ever erase: a loose-boobed Lil' Kim at the '99 VMAs, Gwen Stefani with braces and blue hair styled like horns, Britney and Justin's matching head-to-toe denim getup at the 2001 AMAs, anything that Fred Durst wore, ever.

The thing is, we're starting to realize that we don't want to forget the worst, because even as implausible as re-loving parachute pants seems now, we might think otherwise in a few years. (Let's hope not.)

BEAUTY CULTURE

 If there's one thing I know about adolescent devastation, it's that it doesn't last long. Of course, when it happens, it feels like a world-ending moment plucked from one of those über-serious episodes of a WB show that has a written disclaimer at the beginning.

So when we got the news that Roller Magic—Williamstown's roller-skating rink and only Saturday hangout for the under-fourteen set—was closing, it was the dramatic fade-out. *Roller-skating deprivation is serious. One in four teens experiences roller-induced depression. Talk to a grown-up today.*

This would soon turn out to be a blessing that would completely shape my identity, because what ended up replacing Roller Magic was a Brooks Pharmacy.

For my best friend Geneva and me, Brooks was a halfway point between our houses. We began riding our bikes there, pockets stuffed with our meager allowances, which we found actually went a long way at Brooks. It was there that we spent hours in the cosmetics aisle, carefully researching every Revlon, Almay, and Bonne Bell offering, experiencing the rush of grown-up satisfaction that came with riding away with a new purple eye shadow compact (Forever Fig by CoverGirl) or tube of lip gloss (L'Oréal's Rouge Pulp) in pockets.

Beauty was big for us because it was a shared experience (one that sometimes led to mono if you were generous with your ChapSticks). We dyed one another's hair, swapped scrunchies, and copied eye shadow colors. For many of us, the beauty routines we established in middle and high school stuck with us through adulthood, which will now always smell just a bit mentholy from Clean & Clear Deep Cleaning face wash or look perfectly dramatic thanks to Maybelline waterproof mascara. Here's a look at Generation Y's best in beauty.

Gen Y Beauty Arsenal

A tub of hot red, pink, or blue for punks.

HERBAL ESSENCES

If you weren't a pink bottle girl,
we didn't want to know you.

Semipermanent dye
that didn't piss off
your parents.

HARD CANDY NAIL POLISH
Shimmery pastel lacquers with edgy attitudes.

Homemade streaks with a sugary aftertaste.

BATH & BODY WORKS
Body mists, gels, and lotions that smelled
like foods and flora.

ROLL-ON BODY GLITTER

Portable shine to be applied to eyes, collarbones, and cheeks, often packaged in shapes like stars and hearts.

Makeup for glam bad girls, with rebel names like Roach, Smog, and Acid Rain.

PLASTIC HAIR BARRETTES

We wore Goody's plastic barrettes molded into bows, poodles, and rabbits as kids, then brought them back to pair with super-straight hair and sourpuss faces.

LIP SMACKERS

Meet a girl's BFF, Bonne Bell. Dr Pepper was a mandatory flavor.

HAIR CLIPS

Simply twist and clip.

STICK-ON EARRINGS

Never mind that they fell off two minutes after application; we loved them as little girls and then again as teens.

Looking like an ice queen was everyone's favorite in the late nineties.

X

SUBJECT	GRADE	NOTES
INTRO TO TOPS (SURVEY): LOGOS, CATCH-PHRASES, AND THE BENETTON RUGBY SHIRT	*B-*	*Relax. Don't do it. And never, ever wear a Hard Rock Cafe T-shirt.*
JHERI CURL	*C*	*Poor judgment.*
ADVANCED FOOT-WEAR/LEGWEAR COMBOS: LEG WARMERS WITH PUMPS	*F*	
TRENDS: GRUNGE	*A-*	
ACCESSORIES 101: SLINKY BRACELETS	*B-*	*Fun, but lacked substance.*
INTRO TO META-ACCESSORIZING: FAT LACES	*B+*	*Fun, but too much substance.*
REMEDIAL DIY: PUFFY PAINT	*D-*	*Remember, just because you can wear it doesn't mean you should.*
DENIM 101: FIRST WAVE DESIGNER JEANS	*B-*	

Excellent progress in the use of oversized gold chains, fishnet, checkerboard, and plaid prints. Needs improvement: mom jeans, hair band regalia, mullets both ironic and unironic.

Y

SUBJECT	GRADE	NOTES
TRENDS I: HIPSTERS	C+	*Lacking in originality.*
FOOTWEAR 101: UGG BOOTS	C−	
FOOTWEAR 102: PLATFORM SNEAKERS	B−	
DENIM:JNCO JEANS	D	*Abysmal effort. See me.*
BEAUTY: HARD CANDY NAIL POLISH	A	
TRENDS II: CLARISSA EXPLAINS IT ALL NINETIES MASH-UP	A−	*Nice use of creativity!*
ACCESSORIES: NERDY-COOL HYPERCOLOR GLOVES	B	

Excellent work on mastering the middle part, frosty eye makeup, and Bollywood-glam à la Gwen Stefani. Needs improvement: boho-chic-gone-homeless à la Mary-Kate, tights as pants, Hot Topic neo-goth getups.

Y VS. X-GIRL

Y One of the best presents I ever got came from my sister's best friend in 1997. It was a care package of cool: two Hard Candy nail polishes in colors I'd never seen before (icy blue and pastel yellow), a mood ring, some plastic Goody barrettes, and a pack of X-Girl stickers. I still have ten or so of those two-toned stickers. They were—and still are—among my prized possessions, and as a teen, I used them sparingly. The first one went up on my bedroom door, and when my mom saw it she said, "X-Girl? Leonora, is this some kind of porn thing?"

Porn, no. But for some style-loving girls of my generation, X-Girl has become a fashion fetish, a cultural touchpoint of great importance. A streetwear line conceived by Sonic Youth goddess Kim Gordon and stylist Daisy von Furth, X-Girl had a short four-year run in the mid-nineties, meaning it really belonged to Gen Xers, and to experience it firsthand as a Millennial was rare. I was lucky because Eve and her friends had rad taste, so I got hand-me-downs, stickers, and trips to the Los Feliz boutique while it lasted. But as a kid, I couldn't tell you anything about X-Girl's agenda or history. Never mind that my first e-mail address was x-girl@gurlmail.com. I just thought it sounded cool.

Y's relationship with X-Girl came a bit later, once the line ceased to exist and we realized, along with our Gen X friends, how sad that was. And of course, X-Girl is undeniably intertwined with Sonic Youth and the Beastie Boys—music you'd be crazy to say you hate. Although if you read interviews with Kim Gordon from 1995, you'll hear her try to separate X-Girl from a musical identity, which is just kind of pointless to do when (a) you're Kim Motherfucking Gordon, and (b) you're being interviewed for a *New York Times* trend piece on record labels and artists producing clothing, which was apparently a big deal in '95. Frank Sinatra came out with a collection of neckties based on his paintings earlier that year, FYI.

But I also suspect Gen Yers self-indoctrinated to the cult of X-Girl because it was a love we could share with cooler, older girls. It now makes us feel as though we understand the memory of the time it captured—a slightly gritty-meets-artsy downtown culture that's now vintage.

Watch MTV's *House of Style* coverage of X-Girl's first fashion show and you'll see what I'm talking about. Set up on a SoHo sidewalk, the spot is a window onto the New York neighborhood in its remaining years as an artist hangout before it started resembling an overcrowded outdoor mall. There are still signs of gritty graffiti, and to mirror that, the only real setup for the show is a sheet spray-painted with the word "X-Girl." It's all very guerrilla-style, DIY, and seems as if the whole thing had maybe been dreamed up the day prior. The show's organizer, Sofia Coppola, who at that time was also working on her equally cool line, MilkFed, explains, "Our friend Marc Jacobs just had a [fashion] show down the street, so we figured while everyone leaves that they can come check this out." *Oh, hi, I'm Sofia Coppola and did you notice I'm standing next to my boyfriend Spike Jonze, and yeah, our friend Marc was having this thing . . .*

That's another thing: X-Girl was dominated by a cast of crossover characters—Sofia, Chloë Sevigny, Mike D, Sonic Youth—that got cool in the nineties and then stayed cool in our books because they were still around and producing great art. Well, that, and because they were cool in the nineties.

JUST A FEW NINETIES CULT BRANDS

X-GIRL

MILKFED

DARYL K

BETSEY JOHNSON

TODD OLDHAM

STUSSY

ANNA SUI

SUPREME

GENERATION X-GIRL

 Recently, X-Girl, the nineties little-sister fashion label to Beastie brand X-Large, recently got a reboot on the fashion social network VFiles, featuring Tavi Gevinson as its poster girl. And I'll admit, I briefly lost my mind with excitement over this news. But after the initial frisson waned, I found myself a little depressed by it. For one thing, there were no ringer tees, no preppy A-line minis, no ill-fitting pants for the seven girls on earth shaped like Kim Gordon—none of the pieces I came to associate most closely with the brand in its heyday. But it's more than that. In the end it feels like the only thing that got revived was the logo: Without the cultural moment that first gave rise to it, the whole thing fell a little flat.

X-Girl was and is so closely tied to the indie music, media (*Sassy*), and DIY cool-kids scene of the early nineties that a lot of the discussions I end up having about it have very little to do with the clothes themselves. Nowadays, as with many nineties phenomena, the experience of the brand feels sort of retroactively mediated by Gevinson and her ilk, youngsters who know it only as history, as vintagewear. And of course that's a good thing: It wasn't just a clothing company but a lifestyle brand that captured a particular moment in time, which is exactly what makes it ripe for such nostalgia today—both by those of us who lived it the first time and by those who didn't.

I liked all of it: the clothing, the store, and what the brand itself represented and accomplished. But I sometimes wonder if not enough attention is paid to the clothing itself. Though you may not be able to tell from looking at the designs now, X-Girl gave the fashion world—and young women—something new. It was the first brand I ever saw that combined the mythology of high fashion with a wearability and price point for real girls. The sensibility was L.A.–meets–New York in the early nineties, and as a recently transplanted New Yorker in Los Angeles, I walked into the Los Feliz boutique and immediately felt a sense of recognition. It was an aspirational brand where the aspiration was not toward wealth or luxury but coolness and youthfulness.

The clothing designs took vintage trends as a starting point—seventies ringer tees, mod dresses, eighties prepster wear—and sort of optimized the fit and design for a totally current-feeling, flattering garment. So instead of wearing an oversized baseball shirt that you'd stolen from your older brother or your skater boyfriend's baggy logo tee, you'd have one that was made just for you, with the right proportions and fabrics. The designers at X-Girl seemed like the first people in the history of the world to really think about how a girl's T-shirt should fit. They eschewed flowy or stretchy fabrications for stiffer, more structured ones that had a vaguely utilitarian feel. They introduced the idea of blending different influences—say, mixing boyish indie rock sensibility with structured, tennis-wear tidiness with a dash of unabashed girlyness—that I think has stuck with me and influences my fashion choices to this day.

But this day is different from that one. That moment in time, a swell moment, no doubt, is nevertheless over, and the people involved have gone on to do other things. DIY is a whole culture now, Kim and Thurston broke up, and street wear and contemporary brands aren't only acceptable players on the fashion stage, they're central ones. As for me, the relaunch of that beloved brand is coinciding with a pledge I recently made to myself to buy only secondhand clothing for a year. So I guess I won't be buying the new X-Girl collection after all. Then again, if I see a ringer from the old days on Etsy, I might just snap it up.

ADVENTURES IN IRONY

YMy brother is not a paratrooper. I know this for sure, because I don't have a brother.

But that didn't stop me, throughout high school, from wearing a thrifted T-shirt claiming otherwise. My "MY BROTHER IS A PARATROOPER" shirt was never meant to be an earnest statement of the truth. It was, in 2001, what we called "random," a word we constantly threw around in a variety of barely correct applications.

In this case, random translated to something between "cool" and "mysterious," but what we really meant was ironic. Irony, of course, would become the basis for the Gen Y hipster movement, which for us began here: with vintage T-shirts that made no fucking sense to us.

The less you understood it and the more mundane and obscure the subject matter, the better. AKRON CANCER RUN '92. CAMP EISNER: SHALOM ALECHEM! BILLY SQUIER "SIGNS OF LIFE" TOUR, '84. PENN STATE COLLEGE OF ENGINEERING.

When I moved back to Manhattan for high school, we acquired these items at a place in SoHo called Andy's Chee-Pees (which, contrary to its name, was shockingly overpriced), where you could also find discarded Members Only jackets, dirty Vans, and ripped-to-perfection jeans. For once, newness was passé and looking cool meant wearing someone else's past. Or at least, feigning the vintage look with whatever was Urban Outfitters' latest ITHACA IS GORGES-esque design.

We gravitated toward vintage because it made us feel older, giving us a direct connection with Gen X. We donned Police concert tees and election memorabilia hoping that you'd notice and recognize how we special young people *got it*. We just prayed you'd never ask.

In high school, I had never once stopped to wonder whether my paratrooper tee was tied to some larger cultural reference. If anything, I had just assumed it had belonged to a twelve-year-old Iowan with a bowl cut named Jimmy who was really proud of his big bro. I'd sometimes imagine that Jimmy was now an NYU graduate and an indie radio deejay, and maybe one day he'd see me wearing his old shirt and we'd fall in love. Drew Barrymore would play me in the movie version.

But when I recently began reminiscing about the paratrooper shirt, I panicked. Surely, Google was about to tell me how unbelievably fucking naïve I am to not know "My Brother Is a Paratrooper" was a famous WWII campaign or lyrics from an R.E.M. song.

I got lucky this time. Search for this shirt online and you won't find it. Neither Wikipedia nor Google nor eBay knows it exists. Which I guess means that for once I did something right in high school.

A LEG WARMER–LOVER'S DISCOURSE

My first fashion memory concerns a matching leg-warmer-and-sweater set. When I say "fashion memory," I don't mean the first time I coveted an article of clothing or an accessory. I mean the first time I had an impulse (one I remember, anyway) to wear something that I was aware was a reflection of the time and its trends. I had wanted things before then, sure—a rather majestic pair of purple cowboy boots springs to mind—but those desires hadn't been a conscious part of any larger fashion movement of the time. They were just things I thought were pretty. That matching set, though, was different.

They were black, adorned with large fuchsia and purple polka dots arrayed in even rows, mechanically knitted from genuine, lustrous 100 percent acrylic fiber. As I survey them in my memory's eye, my mind yells at me unequivocally that they are hideous, yet my heart still feels a hungry tug. Yes, hungry: The sense memory is closest to that of taste, as in I wanted that outfit so bad I could taste it.

That fashion and food were synesthetically co-wired in my brain is weirdly appropriate; many a woman learns to replace hunger for food with hunger for style, to endure deprivation in one area for the sake of reward in the other: *Forgo that donut so you can fit into your favorite pair of pants.* And that they were fused together at that particular moment in history makes even more sense, for that was the regrettable era of fitness-as-fashion.

The year was 1983, and Jane Fonda, Olivia Newton-John, and Jennifer Beals had made it very clear to the rest of us that no outfit was complete without a pair of bulky leg warmers. I don't pretend to understand how it is that one random yet specialized accessory ascends to the ranks of appropriate street attire while another never makes the leap. Jennifer Beals spent just as much time in *Flashdance* wearing a welder's helmet, but no one was walking around in one of those.

What we did walk around in, however, was strange and often terrible: fanny packs, acid-wash denim, stirrup pants, sky-high bangs, frosted lipstick, parachute pants, mullets, pleated khakis—the list is as long as it is well documented. While the eighties wasn't the only decade to spawn weird fashion trends, it was arguably the one that spawned the most. Unfettered by anything like reason or aesthetic taste, the masses seized upon trends without ever pausing to think about whether that pair of Hammer pants was really right for one's body type. Like lemmings, we blindly followed, loved everything we saw, applied a critical eye to exactly nothing. You can't really blame us. It was a brave new world of neon colorways and newly invented synthetic fabrics, and there really seemed to be no bad ideas.

What's harder to countenance is the return of many of these trends for a second go-around with the next generation. In American Apparel and Urban Outfitters stores everywhere, we see resurrections of all our old fashion faux pas, remade and repackaged for the next generation of suckers. And while some of them seem perfectly delightful—Ray-Bans, for instance, are a welcome sight anytime—there seems to be the exact same disregard for anything like taste, the same universal acceptance of the awful with the OK, resulting in youngsters walking around with horrible, spandex-induced cameltoes and neon leopard-print muscle tees. Nostalgia, I guess, makes everything seem beautiful, at least for a minute. And while I can almost excuse the young folk for falling prey to the siren song of a paint-splattered T-shirt now and again, it's absolutely unforgivable when a Gen Xer does it. *What's the matter with you? Do you have amnesia?* I want to demand while shaking them by the popped collar. It's enough to make that sweater-and-leg-warmer set seem like a positively great idea.

An idea, alas, was all they were ever meant to be—for me, anyway. My parents, see, were not the sort of people who bought you something just because you wanted it. Outrageously enough, they felt they needed to see the point in it too, and they were not to be convinced that an unusually sedentary twelve-year-old's life depended on being able to wear itchy, overpriced dance attire. It makes less sense when you consider that these were the very same people who had, in fact, bought me those aforementioned purple cowboy boots. But parents, like fashion, are hard to predict. I was doomed to roam the Earth with cold calves and an unfulfilled dream.

As so often happens when you don't get something you want, my good friend got it instead. Laura, whose dad was the mayor of Great Neck, Long Island (this seems somehow relevant here, though I'm not sure why), showed up at school one day in the selfsame sweater/warmer set from my dreams. But instead of inspiring envy, the sight of her served as a much-needed corrective. I don't know what I was expecting—laser beams shooting out of her eyes, a halo of golden butterflies, a four-part gospel-chorus rendition of Irene Cara's "Flashdance . . . What a Feeling," maybe?—but all I saw was the same pretty but undeniably human girl from yesterday in a matching sweater and leg warmers. And I started to understand that desire isn't just about the object itself; at worst it's how we imagine that our best selves are somewhere out there and obtainable at a department store, and at best ways to play dress-up with things we don't (and might never) own. But either way, it's the wanting, not the getting, that's most memorable. In other words, you can't always get what you want, and often that's precisely what you need.

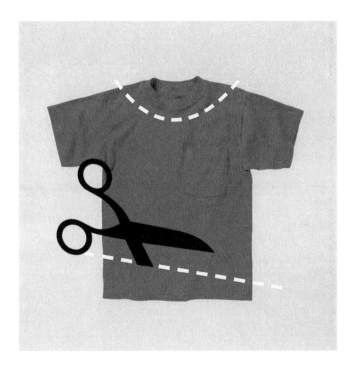

X VS. Y

SEINFELD

THE
MUPPET
SHOW

FAMILY TIES

THE FACTS
OF LIFE

BEVERLY
HILLS,
90210

MY SO-
CALLED
LIFE

FREAKS&
GEEKS

STEWART &
COLBERT

FULL HOUSE

SAVED BY
THE BELL

FRAGGLE
ROCK

DAWSON'S CREEK

TRL

CHAPTER 3
TV

X INTRO

SAME X TIME, SAME X CHANNEL

 My earliest television memory is of losing my shit at the end of an episode of *Sesame Street*. Enraged that my favorite show was over, I screamed, "Bring it back!" at the nearby shell-shocked adults, who wearily explained to me how television worked—a show was on, then it was over, and then you had to wait for the next time it came on. In other words, I was its bitch, and there was nothing I could do about it.

While this information didn't go over too well at the time (cue more screams), it was also essential in building up my attachment to my favorite shows. Having to wait for, anticipate, and then mourn the end of an episode was part of what made you love it. And *so* I loved all of it. Back in the seventies, if you were a kid, your TV options were limited. There was PBS, and there were Saturday-morning cartoons. That's it. You tuned in when your shows were on, you watched them once a week, and that was it. And while this mostly blew, there were some things about it that were awesome. TV gave a sense of structure to the day and the week. It meant that Saturday mornings were sacred—you got up early, crept into the living room, positioned your face approximately two feet from the television screen, and, still half asleep and pajama-clad, quietly gorged on sugary cereal and Hanna-Barbera cartoons.

The very limitations of TV—the fact that it was scarce and anchored to particular points in time and space—were what gave it the quality of ritual. Those limitations gave our favorite shows a hallowed status, the ability to stop us in our tracks and make us zoom home for the opening credits. In some ways, it was a far less social medium than, say, YouTube—you couldn't instantly share something you'd watched, or your opinion of it, with all your friends. But it was social in a different way: You got together and watched things as a group, or a pair, and you talked about what you'd seen during the commercials. Nowadays, this sort of behavior has a quaint, nostalgic quality: viewing parties, which mostly happen in connection with events that still demand to be watched in real time, like the Oscars or the Super Bowl.

Of course, things started to change when VCRs arrived in homes, but throughout the eighties and nineties we still tended to think of TV as something that happened at particular times: From the "Thriller" video premiere to Must See TV, we kept appointments with our programming. It's not that hard to imagine, especially since the networks still cling to these principles and still gauge the success of their shows with Nielsen ratings. But increasingly, we watch TV when we want, on our terms, and on whichever device we have closest at hand. Cartoons are broadcast twenty-four hours a day, seven days a week, and if your favorite show isn't on, chances are you'll find a bunch of episodes on Netflix or iTunes or Hulu.

If TiVo had existed when I was five, it's likely that many *Sesame Street*–related tantrums might have been avoided. But would I have loved the show as much? To have such ongoing and total access to it must, by all laws of economics and common sense, reduce its value in my eyes; to be able, when it was done, to watch fifty other shows to fill the void, must diminish its specialness.

Which isn't to say I don't love TV the way it is now. I do. A lot. The shows are better, and the benefits of being able to watch them on your own schedule and terms are hard to overestimate. (The idea of missing an episode of your favorite show and never, ever getting a chance to see it again sends a chill down my spine.) I love that anyone can become a fan of *The Wire* or *Seinfeld* or *The Mary Tyler Moore Show* whenever they happen to get around to it. TV has become our bitch, and life is all the better for it.

But I do miss those Saturday mornings.

Y INTRO

NICKELODEON NATION AND THE WORLD OF WEIRDOS

There are few things that I love more than television. (And yes, I would go marry it if I could.)

And I know I'm not the only Gen Yer who shares this sentiment— although maybe you guys feel more like you and TV have a platonic or common-law thing going on. The point is, Millennials feel incredibly defined by the television we watched, perhaps more so than any other thing, because TV is never just about who kissed whom or high school hallways. It's a presentation of everything important in that moment—fashion, language, music, current events, hotties—which you got your regular dose of for years on end, much like a Flintstones vitamin.

At the risk of sounding like a broken record (which I hear is like a giant CD skipping), I find myself coming back to the idea of nostalgia and how Gen Y latches on to our past in a way that's becoming increasingly intense. A common conversation we're having is about the window of time it takes for us to label an item from our history as a "classic," which seems to be getting smaller and smaller. Not long ago, my friends were Instagramming a revival event featuring the cast of *The Adventures of Pete & Pete,* and if you feel like watching vintage Nickelodeon, you can now find a TeenNick block of programming called "The '90s Are All That" featuring a bunch of shows from ye olde days. This stuff now makes us feel old, but in a good way.

We don't like to exclude things that keep us tied to our histories, so we'll just as easily pay tribute to the corny programs we watched—*Full House, The Fresh Prince of Bel-Air, Saved by the Bell, Blossom, Boy Meets World, Step by Step,* to name a few. But I think the real reason we cherish Gen Y TV is that we are truly proud of how different some of it was and how we witnessed major shifts and evolutions in style. It's maybe the one advantage we have over Gen X that we can rub in their faces. *Na-na-na-na-naaaa.*

Gen Y has been primed from a young age to be comfortable with worlds full of darkness and cynicism. (Can I get a scowl up in here from all my former goths in the crowd?)

I mentioned *The Adventures of Pete & Pete*, which is already a great example of a story that combined humor with a bleak setup, bringing odd characters to a bland suburbia—Mom, with her signal-receiving metal plate in her head; Little Pete (estimated to be about ten years old in the first season) with a mermaid tattoo named Petunia; and Artie, the Strongest Man in the World.

But even while *Pete & Pete* might have catered to our older sensibilities, we were getting doses of weirdness via traditional kid-friendly formats. Consider the crop of cartoons Nickelodeon began creating in the early nineties: *Rocko's Modern Life* (1993), *Aaahh!!! Real Monsters* (1994), *The Ren & Stimpy Show* (1991), *Rugrats* (1991). There are others that came out of the Nicktoons block, but these stand out the most to me as animated shows that broke out of the Purell-doused norm dominating kids' TV. These new Nick shows were built on surreal, absurdist, and dark humor and set in environments that looked dirty or like bad dreams. *Ren & Stimpy* is an obvious example, but I'd argue that it was actually less sophisticated in the way it abused potty humor and traditional cartoon violence. There was also *Rocko's Modern Life*, whose opening credits were like an acid trip in a Dalí painting. *Aaahh!!! Real Monsters* depicted an ugly world in muted tones with monster characters like Krumm, a hairy and smelly walking piece of naked flesh with no apparent genitalia who held his eyeballs in his hands, or Gromble, a four-legged professor-monster who wore red high heels on each of his feet and sported accessories that could have just as easily doubled as S&M props. In *Rugrats* you got Lil and Phil, twin toddlers who were on an earthworm-only diet and were nearly indistinguishable in their genders, as well as Chuckie, a neurotic baby nerd with some questionable psychological issues.

As we got older (mind you, we're only talking a few years later, but the jump seemingly went from training bra to Victoria's Secret overnight), quite a lot of the TV we watched was arguably similar—it's just that the monsters and oddball characters were drawn into worlds that were more real. The reality shows were essentially all the same show: *America's Biggest Weirdos*. The soap opera–like series tended to have themes of darkness, alienation, and depression. See: *Felicity, Dawson's Creek, My So-Called Life* (which is arguably an X/Y crossover show). And then you had the comedic yet dark and complex *Buffy the Vampire Slayer*.

As we got used to embracing worlds where the glaring imperfections and messiness became comedy, we carried certain things away, which we can see in how Gen Yers present themselves now, both on-screen and off. If you haven't noticed, we tend to rely heavily on extreme awkwardness and dry language—we took these traditionally negative things and made them part of our identities. Take a look at some of the Gen Y characters on TV now, and you'll see the "adorkable" Jess on *New Girl*; Max of *2 Broke Girls*, whose brain is a sea of sexual innuendos and sharp insults; or *Community*'s BFFs Troy and Abed, two *Dr. Who*–obsessed nerds.

And then there's HBO's *Girls*, maybe the clearest example of where Gen Y stands in terms of entertainment. On *Girls*, you'll find self-deprecating characters chasing after humor created by their own humiliation and pity. There's an inverse aspiration aspect at work here, too, showing that the new "city girl having it all" looks messy and cobbled together, is ten pounds over-weight, and comes in drab hues.

Which, when you think about it, is kind of just like *Rugrats*. Except the babies are just a little bit older.

DADDY ISSUES: HOW RUFUS HUMPHREY RUINED EVERYTHING

 No one prepares you for the day of reckoning known as The First Time You See Someone of Your Generation as a TV Dad. Not a dad like someone with a newborn baby. A DAD. Like, with teenagers and a mortgage and sepia-toned memories of his own youthful follies and glories. You know who I'm talking about. He's the guy all the beautiful, knowing young people on the show (aka his children) tolerate and laugh at and pity and rebel against. He's the guy no one is supposed to identify with. No one tells you about the feeling of impo-tence and irrelevance that washes over you the moment you realize that he IS the one you're identifying with.

That is the horrible gift given to me by Rufus Humphrey, the ex–indie rocker father of Dan and Jenny Humphrey on *Gossip Girl*. Oh, his existence wasn't the first blow to my generation's pride; we had already endured such desecrations as the relaunch of *Sassy*. But there was something in the sheer completeness of the portrait—the flannel shirts, the pimped-out vinyl collection, the obscure early nineties band-name-dropping—that struck just close enough to home to threaten the very foundations of my self-image. Like the first time you hear your voice on an answering machine and realize that how you sound in your head is not at all how you sound to the rest of the world, Rufus Humphrey is an all-too-recognizable evil-twin version of Gen X, a funhouse-mirror reflection of our collective identity.

It's not his annoying bouts of self-pity or skeevy man jewelry or even the cringefest of a band name (Lincoln Hawk). No, it's these things in prox-imity to actual coolness—the wedding officiated by Sonic Youth, say—that make him so unnerving. If he were a full-blown caricature, entirely divorced

THE RUFUS EFFECT
TV Dads and the Discomfort They Engender

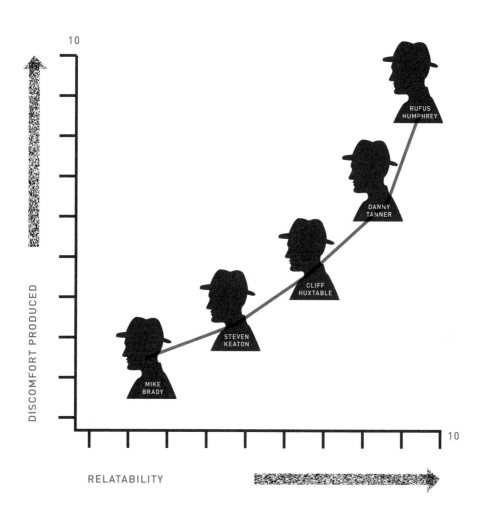

from any true resemblance to persons known, it would be a different story. But there's more than enough reality in there to make the picture function not as unintentional caricature but as unintentional satire, a kind of ridicule that knows its subject all too well and wounds with accuracy and specificity, not broad strokes.

And once Rufus's fictional presence had begun to poison our reality, it threatened to spread, to pollute all our cherished early-nineties memories. If he's buddies with Kim Gordon and Thurston Moore, who's to say he didn't hang out with Kurt Cobain or Paul Westerberg or Ian MacKaye? Where does the insanity end? And I began to see that Rufus Humphrey isn't just a TV character but a disease of the mind.

I'm being melodramatic, you're thinking. Well, sure. I mean, let's put this in context. Is he any worse than Steve Keaton, the ex-hippie from *Family Ties* who abandoned his ideals for a suburban life raising a Nixon-quoting neocon? Um, yeah. Because that guy was old. Rufus is someone I might have dated in college.

Other than that, no. He's not so bad. He's a nice, smart guy whose heart is in the right place, who has problems of his own and an OK sense of humor, who's doing his best to raise decent kids. He is, in other words, a TV dad.

And for that, I can never forgive him.

A CREEK RUNS THROUGH IT: DAWSON'S CREEK AND FIRST LOVE

 When *Dawson's Creek* premiered, I was in seventh grade and caught in a blissful lustcloud of my first "relationship." Greg Mann was the self-appointed Dawson of Pine Cobble School, not because he was arty or into film but because he was blond and wore baggy khakis and unbuttoned plaid shirts. He was generally considered the hottest guy in our class, and having beat out approximately nine other thirteen-year-old boys for the title (it was a very, very small school), he wielded it with a calm ruthlessness that made him irresistible. I'd attracted Greg's attention by trading on my obvious resemblance to

Jen (I was blonde and had moved to our town in western Massachusetts from Manhattan) and unseating the school's equivalent of Joey, a popular brunette and a good friend of Greg.

Our romance started, as many did back then, with a fleeting exchange during a field trip to the Norman Rockwell Museum (ah, how the clichés abound). I'd lost my coveted mocha-shimmer Revlon lipstick, and Greg had been the one to find it. We'd exchanged all of ten words, but that was all it took before we locked eyes again on the bus back to school and, a few rows ahead of me, he mouthed, "Will you go out with me?"

Our relationship was built on a sturdy foundation of watching and talking about *Dawson's Creek*, imagining that our lives were somehow the blueprint for the show, never considering that it might be the other way around or that we hardly came close. On Tuesday nights, we'd tune in simultaneously, and Greg would call me (and a few other girls, I found out later) during the commercial breaks to marvel at the episode's uncanny resemblance to our lives.

I remember the conversations going something like this:

ME: Did you hear the part when Joey was like, "Dawson, your life is a hurricane!"

GREG: And then he said, "No metaphors, Joey!"

ME: I know! That is, like, you.

But a lot of them went like this:

ME: So . . . do you think Dawson and Joey will ever get back together? They *really* shouldn't because that would be a *really* bad idea.

GREG: Yeah, Dawson really likes Jen, so I think they're gonna keep going out.

The weird thing was, while you had to respect Dawson for being the show's main character—making him a total hottie by default—I now fail to recall anyone (myself included) pining after him the way we did for Pacey, Dawson's male BFF. I now actually feel quite bad that I maintained the illusion with Greg that Dawson was top dog, when really, all along, the girls' locker room conversations were squeals and sighs about how Pacey was such a dreamboat. Pacey was supposedly the town fuck-up, born into a mother-less family with a dad who hated him, when in fact he was crazy-smart (even though he coasted on a C average) and was incredibly noble and loyal. He was the type of dude who would actually defend a lady's honor and give a guy a bloody nose if he had to. While we wanted Pacey as a boyfriend, we acknowledged that Dawson was perhaps the guy you come around to and marry in the end, with all of his classic notions of romance.

> **JOEY:** Do you think every Joey has a Dawson and every Dawson has a Joey?
> **DAWSON:** I hope so. For their sake.
> *—season 3, episode 2*

Maybe we were all just in the right place at the right time, but *Dawson's Creek* managed to tap into our hormonally charged psyches like no other television show or movie had done before. At the core of every episode was melodramatic anger and confusion, which might have been standard for any dramatic entity, but it seemed far more real to us because the world of Capeside felt tangible. You'd recognize Jen or Joey sporting cargo pants from a recent dELiA*s catalog, current movies were a constant reference, and I even remember once, Joey pulling out the same *Adventures in Reading* textbook we were using in English class. Considering she was a sophomore in high school and we were seventh graders, this made us feel immensely smarter.

While we felt incredibly sophisticated identifying with these oddly self-aware characters who traded hyperarticulate bons mots ("All right, I'm sorry if my confidence and convictions discombobulate you." —Dawson Leery) and thought a lot about losing their virginity, in retrospect I'm struck by the innocence of *Dawson's Creek* and its characters—especially in comparison to its exponentially more jaded descendant, *Gossip Girl*. Sex was a huge plot driver on *Dawson's*, but the mere fact that it wasn't a default circumstance seems positively quaint today. At Capeside High, its students may have talked like grown-ups, but when it came to sex and relationships they were still kids wrestling with unfamiliar feelings and unmanageable hormones. (By contrast, the characters on *Gossip Girl* seemed like dissolute middle-aged divorcées trapped in the bodies of teenagers.)

CREEK SPEAK

A BRIEF REFRESHER IN DAWSON LEERY VERNACULAR

1

Memorize every SAT vocab word and pepper your sentences with at least two. "Your displays of idiotic jubilation over the Old Navy performance fleece sale only highlight the abundance of superficiality in your small world."

2

Adverbs are your friend: exceedingly, unequivocally, inextricably, utterly.

3

Conversations are never about the trivial matters at hand; always bring things back to life and its meanings. We are born and then WE DIE. If that's a bit too heavy, usually a reference to any type of "vicious cycle" will do.

4

Always invoke the master. One can never go wrong beginning a sentence with "You know, Spielberg once said . . ."

5

Try practicing by filling in the blanks:

Thank you, _____,
(NAME OF PERSON)
for your earth-shattering

rationale. If you had one

_____ of wisdom, you'd
(AMOUNT)
see just how _____
(ADVERB)
screwed we all are! This is

a _____
(NAME OF SPIELBERG, KUBRICK, OR CAPRA DRAMA)
_____ moment;

don't think it's not serious.

WOMEN IN TV TRADING CARDS

MARY RICHARDS

"I'm an experienced woman. I've been around . . . Well, all right, I might not've been around, but I've been . . . nearby."

NAME: Mary Richards
SHOW: *The Mary Tyler Moore Show*
SPECIAL POWERS: Turns the world on with her smile
SECRET WEAPON: Spunk
SIDEKICK: Rhoda the Wisecracker

DENISE HUXTABLE

"If you have 60 percent of a pie, that's still a lot of pie!"

NAME: Denise Huxtable
SHOW: *The Cosby Show*
SPECIAL POWERS: Seemingly endless (and amazing) sartorial transformations
STEALTH SKILL: Heartbreaker

BRENDA WALSH

"Nobody knows me here! I could be anybody. I could be somebody!"

NAME: Brenda Walsh
SHOW: *Beverly Hills, 90210*
SPECIAL POWERS: Fitting in with rich people
PARTNER IN CRIME: Fraternal twin brother, Brandon
WEAKNESS: Dylan McKay

Elaine Benes

"Get out!"

NAME: Elaine Benes
SHOW: *Seinfeld*
SPECIAL POWERS: Serial dating
SECRET WEAPON: Bad dancing
ENEMIES: The Soup Nazi

P·H·O·E·B·E BUFFAY

"Smelly cat . . . it's not your fault!"
NAME: Phoebe Buffay
SHOW: *Friends*
SPECIAL POWERS: Brings goo to the people of Manhattan via massage therapy and horrible son
ALTER EGO: Regina Phalang
NEMESIS: Twin sister, Ursula

ANGELA CHASE

"School is a battlefield . . . for your heart."

NAME: Angela Chase

SHOW: *My So-Called Life*

SPECIAL POWERS: Melodramatic monologues, teenage angst, putting together multilayer classic nineties outfits

KRYPTONITE: Jordan Catalano

---

daria morgendorffer

"We are now entering Hell. Please keep your hands and elbows inside the car."

NAME: Daria Morgendorffer

SHOW: *Daria*

SPECIAL POWERS: Breaks her opponents with biting, monotone sarcasm

SIDEKICKS: Jane and Trent Lane

LINDSAY WEIR

"So . . . you wanna make out or something?"

NAME: Lindsay Weir

SHOW: *Freaks and Geeks*

SUPERHERO CLASS: Freak

UNIFORM: Oversized army jacket

JESSE SPANO

"You macho pig!"

NAME: Jessie Spano

SHOW: *Saved by the Bell*

SPECIAL POWERS: Brains and feminist rhetoric

KRYPTONITE: Caffeine pills

Buffy Summers

"Does the word 'duh' mean anything to you?"

NAME: Buffy Summers

SHOW: *Buffy the Vampire Slayer*

SPECIAL POWERS: Saving the world from vampires, often in periwinkle miniskirts and platform shoes

SUPPORTING HERO: 242-year-old vampire Angel— precarious ally, true love

I now realize how lucky I was to have grown up in the shelter of Capeside High. While my identification with Jen Lindley, the girl who "was moving really fast in New York City," was borderline scandalous at the time, all you have to do is imagine that same character trying to face down Little J at Constance Billard to realize just how wholesome she was.

Of course, the thing about adolescence—and the real reason we love shows about it—is that even the blandest suburb or toniest upbringing can't shield you from heartbreak.

AMERICAN IDYLL

 Thursday nights my junior year in college were holy: For one evening during the week, the revolting couch in the dorm basement relinquished its usual role as a site for late-night hookups and blackout-drunk swoons and became the family gathering spot, the place to watch *Twin Peaks*. Like everything I loved in college, *Twin Peaks* was an occasion to overanalyze, overthink, and obsessively search for meaning where it might not actually exist. Each episode was so rife with possible significance, so overburdened with clues and secret messages, that it kept us buzzing all the rest of the week. "Who killed Laura Palmer?" was our "Who shot J. R.?," the burning question of the day; the problem, of course, was that the longer the question remained unanswered and the more ridiculously complicated the storylines became in order to sustain the mystery, the less likely any conclusion would be to actually satisfy us. And of course, it didn't. Luckily, the fun wasn't in getting the answer but in all the conjecture and theorizing that led up to it. In the end, the central murder of the story was less the point than figuring out what that creepy backward-talking and -dancing dwarf was saying, or where the White Lodge was, or what the significance of owls might be.

This penchant for overanalysis isn't, of course, a trait exclusive to my generation but rather a quality common in college kids of all eras. What was sort of a marker for our generation, though, was the obsession with David Lynch and all that he represented: the weird, the creepy, the quietly grotesque, the incursion of the abject into everyday life, the ever-returning repressed, just-beneath-the-surface rotten underbelly of America's shiny and verdant exterior. At its heart, *Twin Peaks* was a classic soap opera viewed through one particularly weird auteur's lens. Like other shows we loved, it was an example of and commentary on its melodramatic genre—and in case you didn't catch on to that, it gave us *Invitation to Love*, a pulpy soap-within-the-show (much like *The Simpsons' The Itchy & Scratchy Show* or Jerry and George's sitcom on *Seinfeld*) to make the point as unsubtly as possible.

Positioned against *Cheers* on Thursday nights, it was the diametric opposite of that (also great) show: *Cheers* was a near-perfect specimen of the sitcom, with well-drawn characters, hilarious dialogue, and obligatory sexual tension, a paragon of a reliable and unadventurous product. *Twin Peaks* was all adventure and newness, imperfect in the extreme, a genre unto itself.

There was beauty in every shot, filmic mise-en-scène, and artful editing, the likes of which no one had ever bothered to associate with TV before. Along with certain developments on MTV, it reimagined TV as a director's medium, a place where not only stories were told but visions were achieved. Nowadays, the TV auteur is everywhere—J. J. Abrams, Joss Whedon, Vince Gilligan, Ryan Murphy, Alan Ball, Lena Dunham, and many more are considered artists in their own rights, and each of them, arguably, owes a debt to Lynch for carving out this space, however imperfectly.

Anyway, I loved it. I loved its knowing embrace of the genre it skewered, its ability to contain multitudes of humor and melodrama, irony and sincerity. I loved Audrey Horne, the beautiful yet creepy ingénue who wielded her sexuality with the recklessness of an eleven-year-old boy who's just discovered a lightsaber. I loved the blatant absurdities that were nonetheless quaintly reminiscent of small-town quirks—the Log Lady, the one-eyed housewife whose obsession with silent blinds drives her mad—but most of all, I loved Agent Cooper, a throwback of an American hero whose relentless optimism and courtly politesse were all too easy to mistake for naïveté.

The great thing about Agent Cooper was that his wide-eyed appreciation for the wholesome pleasures of Twin Peaks—great pie and coffee, fresh mountain air, small-town manners, and magnificent trees—was in no way tarnished by the discoveries he made about the town's hidden dark truths and mysteries. He was, like the show itself, somehow able to straddle the odd and disconcerting juxtapositions that life invariably entails—the quietly mystical, the bombastic, the mundane, the flawed, the beautiful, the weird, the sublime, and the just plain evil—all the while remaining completely himself, masculine but never macho, unassailably good, and refreshingly straightforward yet on oddly familiar terms with the otherworldly and the sinister.

It was this insistence on a moral center that intrigued and made *Twin Peaks* more than just a thrill-seeking walk on the weird side. The point of Lynch's subversion of America's apple-pie image was not simply to obliterate it but to enrich, complicate, and ultimately reanimate it in a more complex, enduring form—one which vanquished evil not through ignorance or denial but by looking it square in the eye and returning to tell the very strange tale.

I DON'T WANT YOUR MTV
(AND THE FEELING'S MUTUAL)

 Like many of my adolescent liaisons, my relationships with MTV was passionate, on-again/off-again, often confusing, and involved wearing something that I would later regret.

When MTV debuted in 1981, it was like the Twitter of its time: something kids instinctively understood and embraced that their parents could not comprehend. Just as many older folks don't understand why someone would want to read 140-character updates on the brunches and hairdos of their friends and media idols, grown-ups back then couldn't grasp the appeal of a TV network programmed with what were, effectively, commercials. They couldn't fathom the notion that in place of traditional narrative they were now expected to enjoy a three-minute visual fever dream about Simon Le Bon pursuing a part-black, part-leopard "jungle lady" through a fecund tropical setting. It just didn't compute. I remember multiple occasions on which my father walked in, gazed blankly at the screen for a moment, and asked, "What *is* this?"

But we kids loved it, and adopted it seamlessly into our understanding of what music and the music business were all about. We rushed home to watch the next overhyped premiere, argued over which VJ was our favorite, and generally accepted the fledgling network's unstated but highly successful premise: It wasn't a TV station, or not *just* a TV station; it was a culture. The station IDs attested to this, featuring images of an MTV flag being planted on the moon and an ever-morphing logo, animated with wildly different colors and patterns or being spray-painted over the White House. And while people lamented gravely that the era of video relegated the actual music to secondary status, that now seems like quaint overreactive alarmism. Rock and roll had always been a highly visual medium, equal parts style and substance.

What MTV did change, however, was the *nature* of the visuals: As so-called filmmakers entered the fray, music video became a testing ground for all sorts of visual shenanigans. It's hard to believe we couldn't tell how cheesy and ridiculous most of the eighties videos were, filled with split screens and cheap camera tricks and glow-in-the-dark face paint and terrible, terrible hair. It became the de facto space for experimentation with new technologies and wacky ideas, and of course it's the very videos that employed such innovations—Dire Straits' "Money for Nothing," Michael Jackson's "Thriller"—that seem the most dated today. (Weirdly, a-ha's "Take on Me" holds up pretty well in this regard, which is the only possible explanation for why people can't tell what a horrible song it is.) It was only when a new generation arose of directors who really understood the medium and had grown up with it as a part of their cultural landscape, that some truly badass videos started to get made. With Spike Jonze, Michel Gondry, Chris Cunningham, and the like, music video–as–art form finally seemed to hit its stride.

As with so many things, the pinnacle also signaled the end. We didn't know it at the time, but MTV was changing, slowly becoming unrecognizable to the generation who'd put it on the map. Even as we tuned in to the first couple of seasons of *The Real World* and dutifully wrote term papers on the Baudrillardian bingefest it represented, we sensed that the MTV we knew was changing, pulling away from us, and already busy at work wooing our younger brothers and sisters. In 1988 it would have been impossible to imagine an MTV without the music for which it had been named; a mere few years later it was a fait accompli. When MTV founder Bob Pittman told me, years later, that the guiding principle of the business is "Don't grow old with your viewers," it made a lot of sense. If MTV was a culture, it was not a culture of music but a culture of youth. And as youth slowly became a thing of my past, so did MTV.

The end of the relationship came in 1994, the year after I graduated from college. I was living in San Diego at the time, hoping to avoid anything resembling a career for at least another year. To that end, I found a short-term job working for a company called Mandy's Candies, which required me to wear sexy clothes, an old-fashioned cigarette tray, and a pillbox hat and sell concessions at MTV's *Spring Break*, which was filming that year at the area's popular Mission Beach. As I wandered that culturally barren landscape past blaring radio booths and Oakley-sponsored bro packs and gyrating bikini girls, I recognized that I did not belong here. This was not my MTV.

As with all healthy breakups, though, it made sense in hindsight. We had both changed; we had grown apart. And while the *Spring Break* nightmare didn't actually end at all well (I made a total of six dollars that day), it led to the realization that maybe a career wasn't such a bad idea after all. It wasn't too long after this that I packed up my stuff and moved to L.A.—ready, finally, to pursue my own version of the real world.

MTV ME

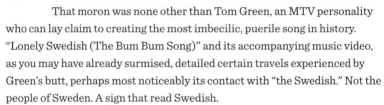

A great moron once said, "My bum is on the rail, bum is on the rail, look at me, my bum is on the rail!"

That moron was none other than Tom Green, an MTV personality who can lay claim to creating the most imbecilic, puerile song in history. "Lonely Swedish (The Bum Bum Song)" and its accompanying music video, as you may have already surmised, detailed certain travels experienced by Green's butt, perhaps most noticeably its contact with "the Swedish." Not the people of Sweden. A sign that read Swedish.

I remember that in the nineties, adults and suited anchormen were constantly wondering: *Is TV completely fucking up our kids?* Their answer was, of course, "yes," and if they'd happened to tune into *TRL* in 1999 to see Tom Green's butt antics, they saw their convictions confirmed.

The MTV of our generation terrified grown-ups and was often blamed as the culprit for all the world's depravities. MTV was killing our brain cells and making us fat. It was getting us knocked up, because they'd figured out a way to create pregnancy by osmosis. Something had to be done; otherwise, President Beavis and Vice President Butt-head would be taking the White House in the next election.

MTV's cast of characters, in the words of my mother, had the "moral wingspans of moths," and while there wasn't a strict "no MTV" rule in our house, it wasn't uncommon at someone else's. In those early years, part of the experience of watching an episode of *The Real World* came with the fear of getting caught. If you were going to take a chance and watch *Spring Break,* you'd best keep a keen ear for signs of parental proximity and a finger poised on the remote, ready to execute a channel change. Back then, our cable provider had MTV on channel 28 and Nickelodeon on channel 27, making the switch from blurred-out body parts on *Road Rules* to a turtlenecked Linda Ellerbee on *Nick News* supereasy.

While I may have watched much of MTV's reality programming in secret as a kid, I'm now not shy to admit that I hold some of these shows—in particular, *The Osbournes, Newlyweds*, and *The Hills*—in high regard as some of the finest lowbrow works out there. I found immense fascination in the documentation of the absurdities of real people. To me, sheer genius is watching Ally Hilfiger on *Rich Girls* have an existential meltdown over burrito ingredients in the supermarket, or seeing one of the *My Super Sweet 16*–ers who *thinks* she has a good body squeeze herself into a slutty thousand-dollar dress while her father watches from the sidelines, crying on the inside. *The Osbournes* spun the lives of fading heavy metal rocker Ozzy Osbourne and his family into a pop-culture masterpiece, somehow managing to convey that even a wacky, famous family who communicates almost exclusively with the words "fuck," "fucking," or some other variation thereof can still stand as an example of an all-American family. Never mind that they're British.

And of course, there's the apex of Gen Y MTV with *that* episode of *Newlyweds* (the 2003 series about Jessica Simpson and Nick Lachey's marriage) giving us what might be the greatest and most iconic moment in reality TV ever in which Mrs. Lachey asks: "Is this chicken, what I have, or is this fish? I know it's tuna, but it says chicken . . . by the sea." Showing us that there are two types of people in the world: those who mistake tuna for chicken, and everyone else.

We logged considerable hours with MTV's Nick and Jessica types—real people who became the network's own characters. They could be already-famous pop stars; they could be nobodies given their five minutes through shows like *Made* or *Road Rules*; B-listers who would become household names à la Ashlee Simpson, Ashton Kutcher, Tila Tequila, Lauren Conrad, and Heidi Montag. Even music (yes, they still had that on Music Television) had its own characters. Carson Daly will forever be *Total Request Live*.

I actually had the opportunity to meet Carson Daly once. I was about thirteen, and my friend Anne's ex-babysitter had moved on to work as a production coordinator at MTV. He'd gotten me, Anne, and Lisa in as part of the studio audience for *Wanna Be a VJ Too*. We spent the better part of an afternoon in a holding room waiting to be filtered in to the audience, and we only got picked at the very end, to line a hallway and cheer as the VJ contestants ran past. For a split second, a corner of my face and half of my yellow hoodie was on MTV. This is my claim to fame, and I'm sticking with it. Despite having to be holed up in a room with nothing to do for several hours, the experience was, like, OMG.

We hadn't thought to bring paper for autographs, so we had to resort to cocktail napkins. We met Carson, who was a total hottie, and he gave us his autograph and even obliged when we asked to try on his baseball cap. A while later, Tyrese emerged from an office, a pack of doves flying behind him as he walked past us in slow motion. The most exciting personality was probably Jesse Camp (remember him?), the first VJ contest winner, who was a beanstalky, wannabe-punk loser who looked like he'd just left a concentration camp and talked like a hillbilly coming down from general anesthesia. He was covered in safety pins and was the coolest dipshit ever.

The term "MTV Generation" is something that's been used to describe both Gen X and Gen Y, and while Yers wouldn't call that inaccurate, we definitely know that there are two factions. Xers may indeed still be labeled the MTV Generation, but theirs was one about giving music a new voice and rebellion so cutting edge that you could actually call it that and have the words "cutting edge" mean something besides douchey PowerPoint lingo. Once Gen Y stepped in, any remaining authenticity of X's alternative framework had been put into our ideological pipe and smoked. Our MTV ran on conspicuous behavior, blunt superficiality, and super drama (usually with blurred-out body parts)—yet because we were unashamed and even proud of it all, it still felt like our voice was there.

Even if all it was saying was "My bum is on the phone, my bum is all alone."

hey

yo

so on "saved by the bell"

yessssss?

what was the main guy's name? jeremy?

oh come ON

are you for real?

something with a j

um. no.

why would i lie

ZACK MORRIS

who is the other guy?

what guy??

ac slater?

screech?

the one who was dating the one played by elizabeth what's her name?

from showgirls

that's jesse spano

 jesse was dating elizabeth berkley?

oh my god i can't even. how are we sisters wtf.

jesse spano IS elizabeth berkley

and she dated slater on and off

 ah ok

which is kind of confusing because she
and him just don't really go well together

 yeah i see her more with Jake.

i mean zack

OMG stopppp

now you are just doing this to get me angry

 and screech doesn't have a girlfriend? ever?

he's in love with lisa turtle. but lisa dated zack
in real life. like the actors dated. off-set.

i mean why do you need to know
this. i mean, you SHOULD know this

 wait but here's what i don't understand. aren't
they supposed to be the cool popular kids?

yes, they are.

so why do they hang out with screech? isn't he like a mutant?

well i think screech has been like zack's best friend from childhood. and everyone kind of tolerates screech. actually, they're pretty mean to him. but somehow it's just acceptable behavior. it really is a testament to zack's good character that he doesn't abandon his friends and because he is cool and popular, he uses his powers for good

oh like marky mark

what? huh? who is mean to marky mark?

marky mark as referenced in clueless. remember he uses his popularity for good. for the treepeople. helloooo?

OH. DUH.

yes. zack morris is kind of like marky marky as referenced in clueless.

ACT UP

SAFE
SEX

"THE
RULES"

SEX AND
THE CITY

DR. RUTH

"SEXTING"

SEXTING

COURTSHIP
VIA TEXT

CHAPTER 4

SEX AND DATING

———

X INTRO

X, LIES, AND VIDEOTAPE

 My earliest memory is of the evening my mother and father told me they were splitting up. There were no blow-ups or noisy crises; they just invited me into their room and told me. And then my mother picked up her already-packed suitcase and walked out the door.

Um, really? In retrospect, it's hard to believe the term "WTF" did not spring into existence at that exact moment. But I wasn't actually alone: It's a familiar vignette for many of my generation. In her smart and wrenching memoir of divorce (both her parents' and her own), *In Spite of Everything*, Susan Gregory Thomas calls it the Important Family Meeting: the announcement that inflicted (or began to inflict) the wound that would emotionally hobble many a Gen Xer well into adulthood. For me, the bomb dropped when I was six and, like any really good bomb, it blew history away. To this day I can't remember a single thing from before that moment.

Like Thomas, I believe my generation was profoundly shaped by our parents' divorces—not just that they happened but how they happened. Like her, I see ways in which it impacted the movies, TV, books, and media we've made and clung to. (You may have picked up on that by now.) But it was in the realm of love, romance, marriage, and divorce that we were, perhaps, most affected.

Divorce and single parenthood weren't just things that were happening in the seventies; they were a huge part of the culture, the sort of sweeping movement that provided journalists and psychologists with endless fodder for self-help books and personal-interest stories. (My dad and I were the subjects of more than one feature about our bizarre life of single fatherhood.) Even kids whose parents didn't split up were somehow a part of it. If you weren't the kid shuttling back and forth between Mom's house and Dad's house or co-parenting your younger siblings in the wake of a parental abandonment, you knew that kid—you were his best friend or mock debate partner or neighbor, and the rhythms of your own life were likely impacted by the interruptions in his. As a generation we grew up with a consciousness of families as inherently fragile, finite things—and this has had the effect of making many of us simultaneously leery of marriage and perfectionists about it.

I, like many of my contemporaries, grew up with very strong feelings about doing it differently or not at all. Until I met my husband, I wasn't particularly keen on the idea of marriage. Like many couples of our generation, we dated and lived together for years before marrying.

The results suggest that this cautious approach to matrimony may be working: We've run with this idea that marriages take work, aren't always easy, and can and should be fought for. We've even extended that model to include divorce as something that can be done well, with the appropriate amount of effort and maturity. When we do split, we forgo the *Kramer*-esque wars of attrition that shell-shocked us as kids, opting instead for cordial mediations and friendly co-parenting arrangements. And, most tellingly, we split up far less frequently than our parents did: Divorce rates have been in steady decline since their peak in 1981.

But while this development seems on the surface to be a victory, there are those who see the situation as more complicated. In her brilliant book *Marriage Confidential*, Pamela Haag characterizes a huge portion of the marriages of my generation as "semi-happy" or "melancholy"—low-conflict, low-stress unions that aren't overtly miserable but tend to end in divorce anyway. (Though I might quibble with the "low-stress" assessment—I don't know about you guys, but I definitely have some stress.) Her point is that we keep trying to fit ourselves into archaic definitions of marriage, preferring to live in unhappiness or divorce rather than try to change our ideas about marriage itself; we'd rather see *ourselves* as broken than question whether it's the institution that needs fixing. I expect Thomas, the author of *In Spite of Everything*, would say that it's because we Xers are *comfortable* with the idea of ourselves as fucked up; we enter into our marriages with our hearts already broken.

This is one area, I have to admit, where I'm more inclined to look to the younger generation for guidance than to my elders. There's something different to me in the way Yers connect, fall in love, and view romantic coupling; they seem less encumbered by the traditions and outdated mores of generations past. They are the first generation for whom the idea of gay marriage isn't remotely scandalous; they don't balk at the notion of nontraditional or nonmonogamous arrangements. It's one realm where I think their oft-maligned sense of entitlement could do everyone a lot of good: When *they* come across something that's not working, they don't meekly pretend they're fine with it and carry on in a state of quiet desperation; they jump in, speak up, demand, and, in the best cases, look for ways to make it better. And while that's the very behavior we Xers like to dismiss as entitled or naive, it's exactly the sort of hands-on redefinition Haag is endorsing in her book: She sees marriage as an outmoded artifact of decades and centuries gone by that's in desperate need of a remodel. "Such institutional dysfunction isn't really tolerated in the private sector," she points out reasonably. "Lawyer Raoul Felder marvels about marriage that 'there is no product in the world (except perhaps commercial Xerox machines) that has a 50 percent breakdown rate, and is still in business.'"

Am I saying that we should just give up and leave it to the next generation to figure out how to reinvent marriage? Is it too late for us Xers? Nah. We may, like our parents and their parents before us, have to admit that we didn't enter into our marriages with all the answers; we may, like our younger friends and siblings, have to do more to claim the institution as our own in some way. And undoubtedly, we will still find that a chunk of marriages just don't work out and resolve to do better the next time around. But that's cool. If those Important Family Meetings taught us anything, it's that we're nothing if not resilient.

Y INTRO

LET'S GIVE THEM SOMETHING TO TWEET ABOUT

Y I realize that in the grand American tradition of losing one's virginity, there may be worse ways to do it than with the movie *About a Boy* playing on the TV in the background. But *still*.

About an hour earlier, Mark and I were in Blockbuster, each pretending not to recognize the artificiality of the situation, as if we were really just *going to watch a movie*. Had that been the case, *About a Boy* would have remained on the shelf. Instead, we just picked something. "Hmm, that sounds interesting," we both said absentmindedly, as if we'd really read the description on the back of the DVD rather than played a game of Blockbuster roulette by picking just any one of those identical blue and yellow cases.

So. *About a Boy* it was. In case you've forgotten, *About a Boy* is the 2002 adaptation of Nick Hornby's novel, which stars Hugh Grant, a bachelor who becomes a father figure to a weird kid whose suicidal mother is played by Toni Collette.

Looking back on it, I've sometimes wondered if there was some meaning behind that choice, some subliminal Freudian thing about kids and families. The fact is, our choosing that movie was totally random. But interestingly enough, it turns out that *About a Boy*—released at the point at which my relationship with relationships began—presents something of a coincidental theme that started characterizing Generation Y's dating world. The movie opens with a voiceover by Grant. He says:

> All men are islands. And what's more, this is the time to be one. This is an island age. A hundred years ago, for example, you had to depend on other people. No one had TV or CDs or DVDs or home espresso makers. As a matter of fact, they didn't have anything cool. Whereas now you can make yourself a little island paradise.

Meaning this: We now had tools that allowed us to distance ourselves from one another. Case in point: Once Mark and I went back to our respective colleges after that winter break, we never really talked again. Unless you count an ongoing war of Facebook poking, which, depending on whom you ask, might be a very meaningful form of communication.

Sex is never simple. There are a lot of different things you can say about how Millennials started doing it, and, of course, everyone's different. But I think we can all agree that our love lives are now completely mediated by technology, both in how we present ourselves to others and in how we interact with them. And between all the texting, social networking, Internet stalking, and online dating (more on that later), it's generally led to what social scientists and ladymags like to call a "hookup culture," a term we rarely ever use to describe ourselves. At least not out loud.

To be honest, it's mostly a nightmare. Here is a poem I wrote about it so that you might begin to comprehend the hollow tragedy that is Generation Y and its concepts of dating:

> **D**inner, rarely.
> **A** "hangout," perhaps.
> **T**exting, totally.
> **I**nternet tells me you suck.
> **N**o response to that e-mail even though you've been Tweeting all day.
> **G**o back to online dating.

I'm sure that Xers have had their fair share of courtship woes, but, in my mind there's a very different flavor to Gen X's world of sex, love, and relationships that feels much more intentional and earnest. I picture Doc Martens–clad kids in the East Village jamming to Salt-n-Pepa's "Let's Talk About Sex," raising AIDS awareness and promoting safe sex; using sex to create an activist identity. Or people actively participating in a dating culture because you'd actually have to make plans *in advance* and *on the phone.*

But it's not as if I'd ask my Fairy Datemother to make it 1990 again. Achieving balance between the traditional and modern is something of a catch-22: The one time I dated a guy who communicated via calls, never texts, weirded me out. Seeing his name pop up on my cell always felt like a surprise and often seemed intrusive. Kind of like that 1998 episode of *Sex and the City* when Carrie gets her first IM from Aidan and she ducks down from her laptop, saying, "Oh my God, can he *see* me?"

Then again, the comfort and well-thought wit that texting has allowed us only works in so many situations. More often than not, you're dealing with what has become the most prevalent, passive, and infuriating text from boys: the "hey." No question. No invitation. No follow-up text. I imagine Gen X never had to deal with this, because how weird would it be to call a girl and leave a voicemail that just said, "Hey." Click.

As for the other stuff like Facebook, Google, and dating sites—these channels can make you feel like you already know someone without even meeting them. The public information that we pull tends to accelerate things in one of two ways. Either you find something you like (e.g., pictures of a volunteer trip, a profile extolling the virtues of Captain Planet) and decide this person is *awesome,* let's get married today, or you see something that rubs you the wrong way (e.g., he's really into Burning Man and/or anarchy) and causes you to conclude that this person is the worst human being ever.

While social networks may give us fascinating clues about the people we're interested in, they're also a huge source of anxiety in dating. Facebook-friend a romantic interest right away, and you risk seeming like you're pushing things too fast. As for breaking up, then you're left with a trail of digital detritus from your relationship, and exes never really leave your lives. (Until you de-friend them. But even then, with enough drunken, late-night determination, it's easy enough to see what they've been up to.) And yet, even with all the new complications and messes, we'd never give any of this up, because there are new layers and opportunities for interacting with people. When done right, a Twitter or Tumblr flirtation can be endearing. The issue is that it's rarely done right because no one really knows the rules when it comes to this stuff. We don't have rules. And even if we did, it would be pretty uncool to follow them.

Technology isn't the only culprit for our lax dating conventions and disillusionment. We had been desensitized to any earnestness for some time. Divorce became so common that to have parents still together seemed like an anomaly. ("Your parents are . . . *together*? Wow.") And each time some pop culture/political "scandal" came up—Janet Jackson's Super Bowl nip slip, Paris Hilton's sex tape, the Clinton-Lewinsky affair—it was treated as entertainment. These things never shocked us. Intrigued us for a minute, perhaps, but after that, who gave a shit? And even when you'd see mushy models of boy/girl-next-door romances, you'd have to laugh, because for every picture of clean-cut suburban sex, you could just as easily find a Britney Spears or *American Pie* counterpart.

Aloofness is what Gen Yers—especially our hipster contingent—do, and it's most applicable when it comes to finding love. With urbanites especially, you'll find they have a difficult time maintaining coolness while pursuing love with any earnestness. To be single and under thirty-five and lamenting your loveless life or openly looking for a relationship tends to make you seem like a desperate sorority girl. What's the rush? Don't you want to be concentrating on launching your app that is totally going to be the next Instagram?

Of course, most of us aren't actually on a collision course with cat-ladydom (even though it may feel that way sometimes). We're still shacking up and getting married. But there's a reason why our romantic image hasn't changed and why people still look at Millennials with the same type of skepticism: because we invite it.

It's come to a point where complaining about the shortcomings of Gen Y dating has become part of our identities. Just as twentysomethings are more adept at creating online personas, some are equally comfortable adding to this an element of open-bookness. We write cryptic tweets that invite questioning; full of angst and ennui, we blog about the difficulties of navigating emotions; we write articles on the Thought Catalog with titles like "Chatroulette Stole My Boyfriend," "The Types of People You Can't Love," or the blatantly self-referential, like "A Memo for Your Twentysomething Apathy." We all want you to see us as Holden Caulfield descendants, caught in a state of perpetual youth and rebellion.

Love, in this way, works in our favor as a sort of commodity. One used by writers as Web fodder. Or by members of indie bands, beloved by the Pitchfork crowd, who tend to write songs about the girls who got away.

In a weird way, it's our most honest way of implying that we need love just so we can get rid of it. After all, the concept of emo can't exist in a state of love. It exists only with its absence.

FIRST CRUSHES: THE WORLD IN ALL HIS FIRE

 My ultimate dream date in 1982 was the following: a quiet dinner with John Taylor of Duran Duran at a candlelit restaurant with rose-filled bud vases on the tables, after which he would take me back to his place and serenade me with the bass lines of all the songs from *Rio* as I fell asleep in the guest room.

I'll give you a minute to cool down.

I was a late bloomer. And I don't mean "late bloomer" by today's standards, which for all I know means waiting until you're fifteen to have a threesome. I mean I *really* took my time with the whole sex thing. Granted, I wasn't in much danger of being convinced otherwise; high school boys weren't exactly banging down my hymen. Regardless, I never, ever fantasized about any sort of actual sexual activity with John Taylor or any of my other media crushes. I imagined meeting them, liking them, loving them, and being

GaryColemanJKNamesMike
28 / m / single
Hipsterbia, USA

ABOUT ME

About Me
Artist. Thinker. Time Traveler. Jack of all trades.

Iconoclastic, philosophical, ego-driven, self-perceptive, often written in fragmented sentences and/or all lower-case

I collect antiquarian books and rare '60s soda cans from Malaysia.

What I'm doing with my life
Graphic design and other stuff. I'll tell you more over craft beers and street tacos.

I'm too cool for this part of the profile

The first things people usually notice about me
My invisible snowsuit

"Funny" yet non-sensical reference

The six things I could never do without
-Oxygen
-Water
-Food (tacos)
-Coffee, French press
-Internet
-MacBook/Everything

Wiseass responses

Truth

I spend a lot of time thinking about
youtube.com/dfwalskiwfe
If you don't understand this, then don't bother messaging me

Link to obscure New Wave film clip

On a typical Friday night I am
Galavanting. Checking out local bands or playing with my band (link to website).

"On a skype call with Vegas"

Sepia selfie with completely unnecessary but supposedly "cool" reference

"At Coachella with friends"

Impossibly pretty "friend"

"Brewz 'n bitches"

Beer

Dog

LonelyGentleman4U
43 / m / single
Yuppieboro, USA

ABOUT ME

About Me
Ugh, I hate this part LOL! Oh well here goes...I'm an educated, okay-looking guy. I'm an optimist. A foodie who loves to laugh! I should warn you now, I can be quite the wise-ass!

What I'm doing with my life
I don't want to buy, sell or process anything for a career. (JK! That's my favorite quote from "Say Anything.") I love my job and I'm very, very good at it.

The first things people usually notice about me
My smile. Also some people think I look like Henry Rollins LOL

The six things I could never do without
-The films of Martin Scorsese
-My rescue dachshund, Alexander Haig
-The outdoors
-My iPad
-Thunderstorms
-Good food and wine!!!!!!!!

I spend a lot of time thinking about
What we'll do together when we meet! I'm a romantic and I crave true intimacy and connection.

On a typical Friday night I am
At home, listening to records on my '74 Technichs SL-120 turntable. Or out trying a new restaurant.

"On my motorcycle"

"Last Saturday"

"at Yosemite"

loved by them; I imagined romantic scenarios like dates and proposals; I never even thought about whether they had genitalia or desires of their own.

Early crushes, for late bloomers, aren't really about sex, per se, but about having an object through whom to start forming an identity around the *ideas* of sex, romance, and love. It's an exploration on the outside that facilitates exploration on the inside, and as such demands varied and continuous input. Which may explain why my earliest crushes, as a child, formed a sort of crazy person's Who's Who of the seventies and early eighties: Eddie Murphy, Jason Bateman (then appearing on TV's hit show *Silver Spoons*), John Travolta, David from *Sesame Street*, and Akira Hibiki, a character on *Yuusha Raideen*, an anime show that aired on the local Japanese TV station in New York in the seventies and was about a giant robot from space (naturally).

As you can see, I really took the notion of unattainability to the next level, targeting not only celebrities but also fictional, animated characters of foreign, short-lived TV series. I liked the safety such physical impossibility conferred, the assurance that there was absolutely no connection between the desire I felt and any possible return. In any case, it's quite a roster, I'm sure you'll agree.

As I got older, my attachments grew more focused and predictable. The male ideals my friends and I worshipped were mostly musicians, and mostly ones in the glam, new wave, or pop traditions—which is to say they existed on a continuum at one end of which was asexuality, the other overt femininity. Like this:

ASEXUAL ·· FEMININE

MORRISSEY	DAVID CASSIDY	PRINCE	BOY GEORGE
	DAVID BOWIE	JOHN TAYLOR	GEORGE MICHAEL
	MICHAEL JACKSON	JON BON JOVI	

In short, it wasn't at all weird back then to regard waifish men with long, moussed hair and lots of makeup and "accessories" as sex symbols; eyeliner was pretty much the bare minimum in those days. We weren't the first generation whose teen idols were accused of being "girly" by their dads, certainly, but we took the tradition to new, extravagant levels. Whether this preference signaled a culture-wide same-sex curiosity or simply a healthy new fluidity in gender identity, I don't really know, but I'm pretty sure the overt femininity of many of these guys made them feel a safer, more relatable option for those who, like me, remained squeamish about sex well into the tweenage years.

Which isn't to say my feelings lacked intensity. It's easy from this hoary vantage point to dismiss those young stirrings, and in truth most of them were pretty benign. But if I really cast my heart back, I can recall the truth of that real first love, the one I felt so long ago for John Taylor, and I can't deny it was a powerful, if ridiculous, thing. While it wasn't overtly sexual, it had all the attendant hallmarks of something sexual: unfulfilled yearning, pain, frustration, desperation, loneliness, sorrow, hope.

And sometimes, when I hear the opening synth sequence of "Save a Prayer," I can picture a fedora'd John in that Sri Lankan landscape like it was yesterday, and I miss the ridiculous, outrageous intensities of my first crush. "Longing, we say, because desire is full of endless distances," wrote poet Robert Hass. And never was there more longing—or more distance—than in 1982.

FIRST CRUSHES: THE NINE-YEAR-OLD-HIPSTER, THE HEARTTHROB, AND OTHERS

THE NINE-YEAR-OLD HIPSTER

There were several eligible bachelors in Mrs. Kavanaugh's fourth-grade class. Despite the fact that this particular group of nine-year-olds committed unforgivable fashion crimes—Teva sandals with socks!—many would turn out to be ambitious, athletic guys who would attend top-tier colleges. The one who caught my eye wore a different type of footwear, and I know this because we played our fair share of footsie. Seamus O'Shamrock (not his real name, but something super-Irish) wore black and white-striped Adidas, which he left unlaced on purpose. He also wore his T-shirts inside out and backward. That's what he was known for; he'd done it once, and it had kind of become his thing. Seamus wasn't trying to be an iconoclast; he was attempting originality. He might have been the first hipster of our generation.

BILL NYE THE SCIENCE GUY

I realize the disturbing implications of this one. But as one of my very first crushes, at around age eight, I fell in love with Bill's brain. To me, he was the smartest person in the entire world.

THE CAMP CRUSH

There's really not a lot I can remember about this dude other than in the summer of 1996 he became known at Camp Eisner as "The Purple Michael Jackson Guy." This was because at the Shabbat talent show, he'd performed a crotch-grabbing dance to Michael Jackson's "Beat It" and in the process had either become so nervous or so pumped up that his face turned a shade of purple. His performance received mixed reviews; I thought it rocked.

THE ARTSY SENIOR

I happened to go to one of those high schools where popularity had little to do with sports; you could be one of the cool kids and still be a bookworm, drama nerd, or tortured artist. Sadly, I was all three and never figured out how to climb the ranks. Joel was into drawing and painting, and he was really quite good at it. He could do stuff like wear a sleeping bag to school, and people would think it was the greatest thing ever. I'd managed to come into his periphery thanks to a short-lived friendship I had with a senior girl (I was a freshman) named Shazz. A friend of Joel's, Shazz was this awesome British punk-raver girl with crazy bleached-blonde hair, a million pacifier necklaces, and a solid uniform of parachute pants and platform sneakers. She was high all the time and almost never came to school, and for some bewildering reason she had decided to let me hang out with her. I also liked her because sometimes she'd have this matchmaking agenda—knowing I liked Joel, she'd invite me to sit with them, and she'd even planted the idea in my head that Joel was going to ask me to prom. He didn't. He went with Shazz. I hate you, Shazz.

LEONARDO DICAPRIO

Obviously. There's no disputing the love I felt for Leo. You can find the evidence in my diaries in which many an entry was signed off, "P.S. Leonardo DiCaprio is sooooooo hot."

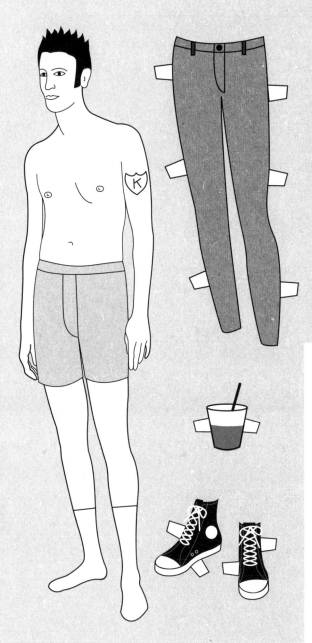

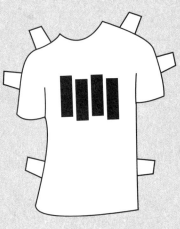

ROCK DUDE

APPEARANCE
spiky hair,
tinnitus,
Black Flag T-shirt,
K Records tattoo (*just like Kurt Cobain's*),
vaguely Neanderthal stance,
calluses,
skinny jeans,
Chuck Taylors

HABITAT
Hollywood

DAY JOB
Graphic designer

IRONIC CATCHPHRASE
"Hello, Cleveland!"

DRINK ORDER
Jack & Coke

RIDE
Honda Prelude

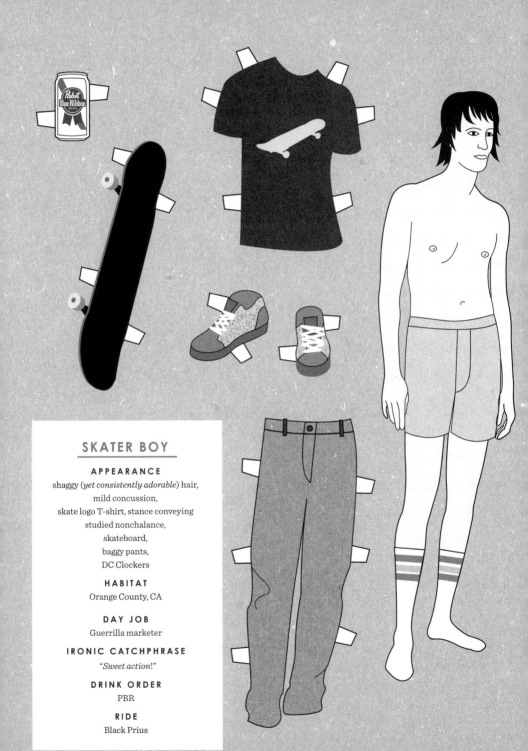

SKATER BOY

APPEARANCE
shaggy (*yet consistently adorable*) hair,
mild concussion,
skate logo T-shirt, stance conveying
studied nonchalance,
skateboard,
baggy pants,
DC Clockers

HABITAT
Orange County, CA

DAY JOB
Guerrilla marketer

IRONIC CATCHPHRASE
"Sweet action!"

DRINK ORDER
PBR

RIDE
Black Prius

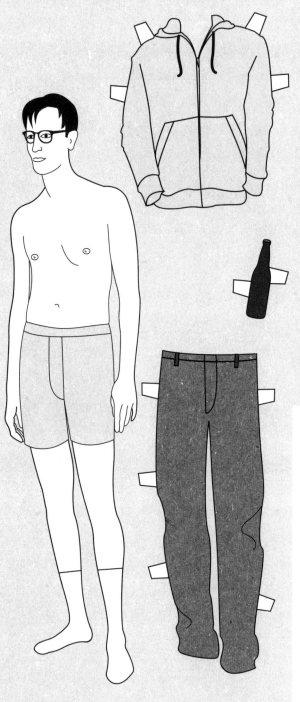

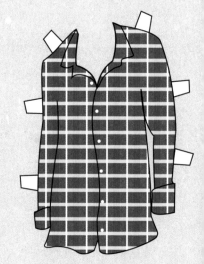

HIPSTER GUY

APPEARANCE
Highly engineered sloppiness,
thick rim glasses,
hoodie,
plaidapalooza in the shirt department,
ever-present scruff

HABITAT
Brooklyn, NY

DAY JOB
Music critic at alternative weekly newspaper

IRONIC CATCHPHRASE
Too cool for that

DRINK ORDER
Craft beer or
his own home-brewed moonshine

RIDE
Vintage Bianchi bike

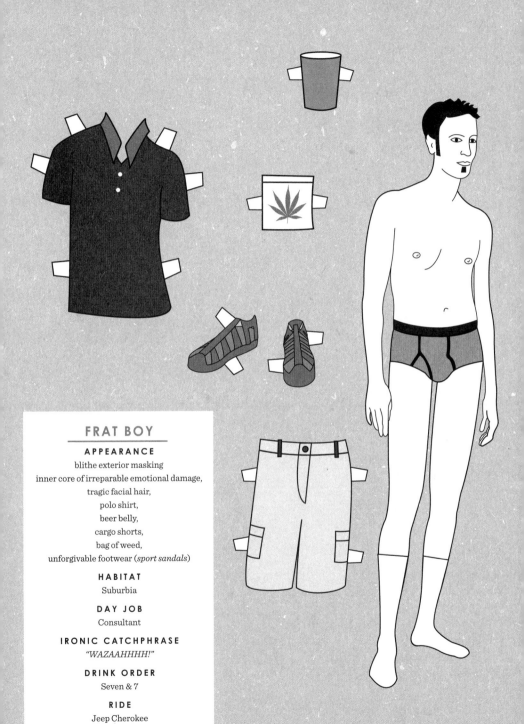

FRAT BOY

APPEARANCE
blithe exterior masking
inner core of irreparable emotional damage,
tragic facial hair,
polo shirt,
beer belly,
cargo shorts,
bag of weed,
unforgivable footwear (*sport sandals*)

HABITAT
Suburbia

DAY JOB
Consultant

IRONIC CATCHPHRASE
"WAZAAHHHH!"

DRINK ORDER
Seven & 7

RIDE
Jeep Cherokee

HOW WE DATED

X In my twenties, I hooked up with three guys. Well, OK, it was more like a thousand, but there were three who mattered (besides my husband). The first I met at a Jonathan Richman show. The next I picked up at the Viper Room while on a date with the first one. The third was the second one's best friend (or was until I started dating him). What am I saying? That I used to be a terrible person? No (but yeah). I'm attempting to illustrate that in the absence of a better way, meeting people was hard. We were reliant, by and large, on work, other people we knew, and bars. Mostly bars. Unlike today, where you can instantly access an online smorgasbord of possible mates filtered by age, geography, religion, taste in movies, and mustache style, we were forced to settle for whoever else felt like being at the Pavement show that night, and it too often showed in our choices.

None of this is to say that people don't still meet and hook up in person; of course they do. But the heyday of bars as ground zero for the dating life, which began in the seventies and took us through the nineties, seems to be over. Gen X movies are full of vignettes about the Darwinian dynamics of the singles scene, from the "how about them apples" line in *Good Will Hunting* to the "scared bunny" sequence in *Swingers*. It was a jungle out there, and we all had an arsenal of worst-pickup-lines stories and tales of flubbed flirtations to get us through the absurdity of it all.

We Xers did the bar scene the way we did everything: with an unhealthy dose of irony and sheepishness, our way of signaling that oh, yes, we knew it was cheesy and ridiculous that we were all reduced to hitting on each other over Zimas and guitar feedback, but what else could we do? We hated the idea that by simply being there, we were somehow aligned with the image of the self-styled pickup artist as personified by Steve Martin's "wild and crazy guy." But our generational quest to be original, to thwart expectation and the norm, was perpetually stymied by the leveling force of longing; there are only so many ways to buy someone a drink or start up a conversation, and every single one of them is an acknowledgment that you're there to meet someone, that you want something from them, which in our behavioral lexicon was just sort of uncool.

Internet dating has changed a lot of this stuff. It forces users to openly acknowledge what they're doing (shopping for a partner), and I'd imagine that it opens you up to a more varied social experience.

With apologies to my exes (and my husband), there's something strangely similar about the guys I dated. They almost all worked in the music industry or as music journalists, which isn't surprising considering I met many of them at rock shows. And while you could argue that this was a reflection of my own interests as a young person and therefore a valid indication of compatibility, I'd say: eh. For one thing, I had lots of other interests besides indie rock back then, but those other interests didn't come with a built-in drinking scene. Even things people take for granted today—being able to seek out a fellow foodie or animal lover—were tough to accomplish back then.

For another, a single common interest is hardly enough to ensure the success of a relationship; as I've grown older I've come to recognize that while shared musical tastes can certainly be a nice thing, they aren't exactly the bedrock of a long-term commitment. When you're arguing about money or suffering through a dry spell or wanting to murder someone for leaving the wet sponge in the bottom of the sink *again*, blasting Lee Hazlewood's "You Look Like a Lady" is not the fence-mender you'd think it'd be. Anyway, most of those guys have moved on from their careers in the music business anyway—including my husband, who quit his job as a music editor just three months after I met him, in order to pursue his current career as a filmmaker.

Would we have started dating if we'd met each other online? I think so; I can easily see him having the sort of profile that'd tip me off to his prodigious intelligence and sense of humor, his preppie adorableness, his amazing taste in television, and his impressive education. But there were quite a few guys I dated in my twenties whom I'd have probably ruled out based on their dating profiles (and a few who would've ruled me out, no doubt). I think I'd have spotted some of the pretentiousness, ignorance, or arrogance that lurked behind their handsome exteriors. Moreover, I might have cast a wider net in other ways—sought out people who lived in different neighborhoods, had other interests or values in common with me, or simply looked cute and funny.

Sometimes, looking at how technology has informed the way people meet today, it's hard to believe we ever got by without the current methods. But much the way we once wrote term papers on typewriters and met up without the aid of cell phones, we made it work. We found each other. We met, we married, we started families, we stayed together against great odds or broke up and did it all over again. And in that way, I guess we were pretty much just like everyone else. Which, of course, drives us crazy.

OKSTUPID AND THE REST OF THOSE DATING WEBSITES YOU TOTALLY DON'T BELONG TO

You Here is a probability equation for you to contemplate:

> Leo has been in love four times. If three of those relationships were initiated through an online medium, what is the probability of her meeting someone offline?

a) 1   b) 25 percent   c) LOL   d) <3

If you selected b), 25 percent, you are incorrect. The correct answer is actually e), none of the above. To be fair, the problem above is something of a trick question because it doesn't account for a number of hidden factors. One has to factor in the prevalence of apathy (subtract .5), the middle school dance–like vibe of bars populated by Millennials (divide by 4), and the death of chivalry (multiply by the square root of pi). Nor does it account for the passage of time and the rate at which members of the human race decide to cancel their JDate memberships. Also, considering that the problem implies that Leo is no longer in love, we are left with a success rate of 0, so now how can we reformulate so that the sum of these two matrices equals Love-squared?

I don't know! Screw you, math.

To put this in layman's terms, I don't expect to be finding love anytime soon, online or off. But, if I did feel like pursuing love, the only way I could actively do this would be through any of the thousands of "computer dating chat sites" (as my mother calls them) out there. I've been a member of Match, JDate, Nerve, HowAboutWe, Chemistry, and I'm sure a half-dozen others I tried for about five seconds. But the Web is an amazing place where you can find romance-oriented communities for whatever floats your MacBook: FarmersOnly.com, Vampire Passions, The Atlasphere (for Ayn Rand fans ... shudder), ChristianMingle, VeggieDate, SaladMatch (apparently there is such a thing as someone who "really loves salad"; I'll believe it when I see it), Geek2Geek, 420 Dating, the list goes on.

But nowadays, the place many a Gen Yer turns to online date is OkCupid, a site that positions itself as young and cool, sort of like the MySpace of dating. Now, I know you're thinking that the words "MySpace" and "cool" no longer belong in the same sentence together (and I agree), but considering that OKC launched in 2004 and started to gain traction around 2006—a time when MySpace was still enjoying a relatively important place on the net—OkCupid did a good job of capitalizing on that youthful flavor. OkCupid hasn't changed that much in its image or vibe over the years, and so you'd think by now, we'd have condemned it to share a cell in the Internet dungeon with Jeeves, but it's managed to remain our only non-corny, marginally viable path simply because there is nothing else out there.

And yet, OkCupid has espoused a digital dating culture that is remarkably well-defined, one that feels so incredibly specific to a certain crowd and era. Millennials use OkCupid, but we don't adore it. Rather, we're repulsed, grossly fascinated, and, on the rare occasion, turned on by a cute bearded individual with glasses who likes the Black Keys. Never mind that you've already been on three supremely shitty dates with copies of this same dude.

From the female perspective (the more interesting one, obviously), OkCupid has two sides: It's half hipster vanity project, half total fucking freak show. I have mixed feelings about OKC ("it's complicated," if you will), because despite the insanity, this is the place where your friends of friends are likely to be found, and that's cool. I've often had the experience of walking around Silver Lake—my 'hood and "America's Best Hipster Neighborhood," according to *Forbes,* because those people really know their hipsters—and racking my brain as to how I know that jean-shorted guy only to realize that I don't; I'd just checked out his OKC profile a few days ago. So, OkCupid can provide a sort of false sense of familiarity when you're hunting down locals. And I must credit the site with matching me with two fantastic people—one of whom I seriously considered marrying, another who grew into a great friend.

But even when you ascribe to OkCupidism with good intentions, you find certain uncomfortable habits emerging. The first is that we're all liars. The more obvious methods of lying aside, the one that gets me the most is how we're all pretending we don't do online dating. We're here, people; let's just admit it. Your Harry Potter invisibility cloak doesn't work online. And yet, people still don't really like to acknowledge that they have an OKCupid profile out there, and if they do, they say something like "It's just, like, whatever, you know." Why do we sign up to play this game we don't want to play? Ever notice how no one ever says, "Online dating is the best!" And of course, the inevitable first Internet date conversation is about "how bad it is out there" and how you "don't go on that many dates," but "I mean, you're different."

Sometimes, you say "you're different" to someone on a first date because you think you mean it. Hey, after all, this guy admitted to a love of bad nineties sitcoms, says he's close with his family, and has a really cute cat, so that all definitely means he's a good guy. More often than not, a first date proves that even a "good" profile isn't a measure of how you'll get along with someone. But for some reason, that doesn't make you any more open-minded about the people who approach you online; it actually has the opposite effect of making you incredibly dismissive and judgmental to the point where the littlest detail can turn you off. You might find yourself reading about that nice Jewish boy until, oh no, he's got plugs you could put your wrist through. Or he doesn't know the difference between "your" and "you're." Or he capitalized the word "outdoor." Or he's wearing a tank top. Nonironically. Or his pictures are all of him in scary clown makeup. Or his screen name is asiantom, hairy-jew, or eatspoopregularly.

So, OK, maybe you can see what I'm dealing with here, and I've included some further evidence (see figure 1, page 114).

Of course, OKCupid isn't all Gen Yers. You'll find your fair share of Gen Xers and even baby boomers on there, too, but in conversations with my Gen X sister about the site, I can tell that she's beguiled only by what are the most obvious displays of my generation's eccentricities. I've generally come to a place of acceptance; this is what it is. But for her, the stories only fill her with anxiety and complete disbelief that any of this exists (see figure 2), and the way she puts it, I see her point: "Jeez, these guys are all so active. They all say something like 'If I'm not halfway up a mountain then I'm probably planning a rave with my fifty best friends and making bacon whiskey.' "

So while I'm not exactly thinking, *Mmm, bacon whiskey*, I *am* thinking I'll at least try anything once. Because you have to hold out hope that one day you'll find something that doesn't just taste OK, but is in fact great.

i sort of like this jewish english dude

despite the fact that his first photo looks like a tranny? he seems ok i guess.

he's kind of cute

and v ambitious

short

cute pic with children

i like him

omg jewish boy is IMing me

omgomg!

tell me something funny to say

 i can't, i'm scared

cheerio?

top o the mornin?

nooooooo

just out of the blue he IMs you?

that is nutrageous

yes

except now he just stopped.

oh wait, now he is telling me a joke . . .

 go out with him.

omg i might love him. he says, "i just got back from new york. was doing passover"

 cute

but then he just said . . . i have to take my dog out. we could continue ON THE PHONE

i didn't respond

 oh wow. he's forward

oh wait

i think i hate him

 whyyyyy

i said i was watching the colbert report

i feel confused

he says he hates colbert

god it's such a roller coaster of microemotion

oh wait!

he says just kidding

omg stop

I'm going to have an aneurysm

me too

 go out with him

omg this is so stressful

 i mean, YEAH

go for a drink with him

where does he live

his profile says west hollywood

but he also lists his income

 what is it

which means he can pay for
my helicopter ride to his house

 hovercraft would be better

on the "typical friday night" section on his profile he says:
"Crying inside. Or outside. Depends on the weather."

 yes i like that

FIG.1:
PROFILE EXAMPLES

CATEGORY	EXCERPT
THE "I HAVE EXCELLENT TASTE" MAN	"Now, I just love movies and music. My favorite movies are Forrest Gump, The Matrix, Lord of the rings, Braveheart, Die hard, these movies are so powerful and touching. I only watch great movies like these."
THE TOTAL D-BAG	"I have had loads of white girls. If you are white, unless you are really special, don't bother. I don't mean to be mean or anything but come on, I can get any white girl I want at starbucks. I like japanese girls, because they have culture and are respectful. i also have a thing for blind girls, because they don't judge you according to your looks and I just like the idea that they won't always have an opinion of me."
THE BLAND ENTHUSIAST	"I'm really good at Making you laugh or making you feel like your the only one in the world! I like taking you on a romantic date or a fun Kool date! Outdoor concerts perferably Rock concerts are my faves. Or taking you out on a outdoor bar, lounge is also one of my Favorite places to go."
THE FRENCH JAVELIN CHAMPION WHO WRITES IN THE THIRD PERSON	"Was a French National Javelin champion in the early 80s."

CATEGORY	EXCERPT
THE CONSPIRACY THEORIST WHO THINKS HE IS A GENIUS	"Once in a while I enjoy discussing some of the more eccentric topics and questions this world and universe present us with. Like this: Do you think it is possible that there's a pattern in the stars? By pattern I mean like a connect the dots drawing, where if one were to connect the dots to certain stars it might form a pattern or a shape of sort that would be like a mathematical geometrical proof that the stars were put in their places by someone or something that has/had intelligence (intelligent design). I think I have maybe found the pattern in the stars. I will show it to you, and many things that will amaze you. There are a couple of other really cool things that I will share with you in person, but I don't want to share on here due to copyright concerns."
THE VERBOSE WEIRDO	[After one thousand words in the same section] "(8) passionate dancing -while I'm an armature here, I love it (both flashy partner dancing and solo) and onlookers often pop out their phone video cameras --—I have a tendency to take over the dance floor!"
THE GUY WHO TRIES TO SELL (SORT OF)	"I am good at first aid LOL, and like to dabble in kitchen, also good in out-door enviorments"
THE GUY WHO LIKES VANESSA CARLTON	"Music: Vanessa Carlton stands heads and shoulders above any artist I ever heard. She fills up 85% of my mp3 player, and I am now trying to collect her acoustic performances."

BACK TO
THE FUTURE

CAN'T HARDLY
WAIT

SAY
ANYTHING

GHOST
WORLD

ROMEO +
JULIET

CLUELESS

HEATHERS

THE PRINCESS
BRIDE

LABYRINTH

THE
BREAKFAST
CLUB

MEAN GIRLS

STAR
WARS

TITANIC

CHAPTER 5
MOVIES

X INTRO

I'LL BE RIGHT HERE

"He came to me.
He came to me." —ELLIOTT, *E.T.*

It was the seventies, and things were getting complicated. Truths we'd previously thought of as unassailable and immutable—our parents' marriages, the availability of gasoline, America's moral superiority, the merits of natural fibers—were being thrown into doubt left and right. Suddenly, you had only one (real) parent and were wearing a polyester jumpsuit and keeping a rock as a pet, and the world was just, like, very confusing.

The films of the era reflected such evolving realities, paying tribute to the complexity of modern life. As kids we absorbed these changes in the medium, even if we didn't see all the films that were transforming it (I never saw *Saturday Night Fever* or *The Godfather* in the theater, but they are somehow inextricably a part of my personal film history nevertheless). A new kind of movie star had emerged—Jack Nicholson, Dustin Hoffman, Billy Dee Williams, Al Pacino, and Robert De Niro—along with filmmakers like Woody Allen, Roman Polanski, Francis Ford Coppola, Hal Ashby, Martin Scorsese, and Robert Altman, who were defining new sorts of protagonists and narratives: less wholesome, less WASPy, more ethnic, more neurotic, funnier, darker, weirder. Hollywood went from being a glamour machine to a looking glass, depicting a far more recognizable world full of oddity and neurosis, danger and moral relativism, self-deprecating humor and senseless violence.

At the same time, the movies we *did* see, movies for kids, got bigger, weirder, and better in the seventies and early eighties: *Star Wars, Jaws, Superman, Willy Wonka & the Chocolate Factory.* We even got a filmmaker to call our own: Steven Spielberg, whose *Close Encounters of the Third Kind* and *Raiders of the Lost Ark* gave us glimpses into a mind still feverishly possessed by childhood visions and began a love affair that would peak with *E.T. the Extra-Terrestrial*, Spielberg's tribute to his own single-parented youth.

E.T. came out in 1982, just as the seventies auteur era was giving way to the high-concept, plot-driven 1980s. I was eleven, teetering on the

brink of adolescence and John Hughes. I probably thought I was too old
for aliens and spaceships, but I wasn't. E. T. differed from the other movies
I'd seen and loved, all of which featured adult protagonists (yes, including
Grease: Olivia Newton-John was thirty in 1978); it centered on a very real
kid in a very recognizable setting, a single-parent household in a suburban
development. Mom is sad and overextended; the kids are obnoxious, rowdy,
hilarious, and hurting from the absence of their father. The main character
isn't a messianic Jedi knight or omnipotent superhero but an ordinary ten-
year-old boy, the middle child in a household with not quite enough parenting
to go around. Like so many kids of my generation, I recognized myself in
Elliott—that feeling of being extremely ordinary yet somehow special, that
too-young awareness of a parent's loneliness, that ever-present awareness of
one's own, that yearning for connection and recognition. In the other movies
of the day we might have found useful metaphors in the struggles of Indiana
Jones or Princess Leia or Superman, but in Elliott we saw ourselves.

People who argue that E.T. is himself a messianic figure have a point,
but not one I agree with. E.T. is an analogue of Elliott, a lost guy looking for his
people, scared and out of place. He's probably just a regular dude back on his
home planet, where everyone's fingertip lights up, and building intergalactic
communication devices out of common household objects is child's play. If
E.T. is a savior, he isn't the divine kind: He's a friend, a playmate, becomes the
conduit for the most human of emotions: compassion, empathy, and love. His
legacy (in addition to those reanimated flowers) to Elliott's family is their
own strengthened connection, the subtle change in older brother Michael
from tormentor to protector, in Gertie from pesky kid sister to gleeful
coconspirator, in Mary from put-upon victim to real parent. To me, the movie
is about finding your people, whether several galaxies away or in your own
backyard, and rising to the occasion when shit gets real.

It was also, as I mentioned, the last film of the sci-fi fantasy genre
that I'd allow myself to enjoy for quite a few years. From there it was onward
to *Sixteen Candles* and other movies that gave guidance for how to survive
adolescence in the eighties (the secret had something to do with having plenty
of hairspray, ankle boots, and a potty-mouthed, quirkily attired best friend).
But *E.T.* was the perfect movie to give me that send-off: It was both a farewell
to childhood and an impassioned plea to carry it with me, and I did. After all,
it came from someone who knew what he was talking about.

REW; FF

 Y The only tangible evidence proving karma's existence might be those BE KIND, REWIND! stickers you used to find on VHS rentals. According to that logic, those who didn't rewind were bad people. Until those separate high-speed rewinding decks came around, the chore could be pretty inconvenient, and more often than not, you'd only get halfway through (or forget entirely) before having to run out the door to make the return. You'd think it really wasn't that big a deal until, inevitably, someone else did the same thing (BE A DICK, LEAVE IT BE!) and you'd jump in right when Willy was being freed. Although to be fair, the title *Free Willy* kind of gives it all away anyhow.

Despite the slightly more involved process movie watching entailed in the nineties—both at home and in the theater—the tradition and ceremony now feels slightly lost to me, and as a consequence, I don't enjoy the same comfort and magic movies once provided. Technology and time has turned me into something of a grumpy old man. The privilege of being able to see most any film for free online, in the comfort of my own home, tends to outweigh my desire to sit in a room full of strangers, which totally makes me one of those Gen Yers who prefers Facebook interaction over IRL. And then there's the internal monologue I get while staring at an eighteen-dollar ticket price that's disturbingly Walter Matthau–like: *When I was a kid, you only paid six bucks for a movie! Highway robbery!*

I'm not longing quite enough to return to the way we once watched. At most, Gen Yers might collect VHS tapes as memorabilia, but I think we're all pretty hooked on the facility that devices and services like TiVo (bo-doop!), Hulu, Netflix, Apple TV, and, uh, "other resources" have given us. But there's no denying the importance of video and movie culture in the experience of growing up Y.

To wax nostalgic (at the risk of sounding like a history lesson from the future): In the 1990s and early 2000s, TV gave us rituals. There was TBS's *Dinner and a Movie* where you could watch *Spaceballs* and get a tutorial on how to make "May the Borscht Be with You" or "Bumpin' Grinders," inspired by *Dirty Dancing*. (Never mind that no one ever actually made these dishes.) In the summer, there was "Christmas in July" to look forward to, when the networks would air marathons of holiday movies.

Weekends usually kicked off with a trip to the video store, refining the art of picking out the best two options, where, inevitably, a cute, Dawson Leery–like film nerd worked. In this way, your tastes were often on display, earning you either approval or complete embarrassment. Although this happened a number of years later, I'll never forget the summer I discovered *Sex and the City* (we never had HBO) and became totally addicted to the point of having to make multiple daily trips to the video store. There came a point when the guy working there could pretty much time my comings and goings so that he'd have the next few DVDs already sitting out on the counter when I came in, and in a humiliating, wordless interaction, I'd pick them up and scurry out the door. I was *so* that girl.

There's not much too different in Gen Y's participation in the grand American tradition of going to the movies. Like most everyone else born after the year 1930, it was one of the main components of our social lives; I suppose it's just a matter of engaging with different films with different groups of friends. The most epic example in many a Millennial lady's life would be counting the multiple times she and her girlfriends wept together over the tragic/beautiful ballad of *Titanic*'s Jack and Rose. Destruction, slasher, and bad Vin Diesel movies you saw with boys. And if you were a nerd, you waited on line opening night (often in costume) for every new *Harry Potter*, *Lord of the Rings*, or *Star Wars* prequel release.

Of course, there were occasions you'd go to the movies with family, which, after the age of twelve, is really not a good idea. There was that time when (for reasons that now escape me) I asked my mother to accompany me to see *Austin Powers: The Spy Who Shagged Me*, which went something like this:

> **AUSTIN POWERS:** Do I make you horny, baby? Do I make you randy?
>
> **TWELVE-YEAR-OLD BOYS BEHIND US:** Huh huh huh, ha ha ha!
>
> **MOM:** OH GOD, LEONORA. DO YOU THINK THIS IS FUNNY? DISGUSTING!
>
> **ME:** [*Shrinks down in seat, hopes to disappear completely*]

Although nothing will ever top the time Mom saw a preview for *Erin Brockovich*. There's a part in the trailer where Julia Roberts goes, "By the way, we brought that water in special for you folks," and seized by such a display of female empowerment, Mom stood up and shouted, "Yes!"

And while at the time, I wanted nothing more than to fast-forward through that moment, there's now a certain joy in rewinding and watching everything all over again.

RADICAL DOUBT: LISTENING TO *STAR WARS'* GEN Y CRITICS

"I find your lack of faith disturbing." —DARTH VADER

 Every once in a while, I'm gripped by a horrible, quiet, shameful, terrifying inkling of a suspicion that *Star Wars* might not be as good a movie as I think it is. In case you don't think that's a problem, let me be clear: This is a potentially major crisis of faith that threatens the very fabric of my being and a cornerstone of my generation's collective identity. Why do my friends and I love the original *Star Wars* trilogy so much that our conversations routinely devolve into competitive trivia matches ("Um, excuse me, but the *Millennium Falcon* did the Kessel Run in less than *twelve* parsecs")? Well, for one thing, we were all six or seven or eight when we first saw it, at a time when there really wasn't anything even remotely like it (1977) and in a world not yet inured to a constant barrage of high-def spectacle. Up to then, our cultural life had involved counting to ten with Big Bird and singing along to "Free to Be . . . You and Me." Suddenly, there were massive space cruisers and haughty princesses and giant furry sidekicks and fey robots and epic battles and twin suns on Tatooine, and we were toast from the opening scrawl to the end credits.

But to say that our attachment is purely due to the fact that we were, as an audience of pretweens in a simpler age, an undiscerning and naive population that also, for instance, considered Laughing Cow cheese to be the apogee of human culinary achievement, would be unfair and untrue. *Star Wars* hit us with big themes—themes about young, isolated people, without much in the way of family or friends, who find each other despite vast dis-

tances and evil forces. It's really about a family so completely asunder—dead mom, dad who left before the twins were even born to go rule the galaxy, brother and sister who were flung to opposite ends of the universe to be raised by others—that only amazing feats of destiny could manage to bring them back together. And it did. As the first generation of children to be defined by the massive divorce rate of its parents, we felt their losses and their yearnings. We were charmed and galvanized by the unlikely but durable "blended family" comprising two droids, a Wookiee, a wacky old hermit, a snooty princess, a farm boy, and a gruff smuggler—precisely because that was the type of stability we could only hope our own lives were headed for. That all of it was meant to happen—ordained by destiny—gave us faith that everything happened for a reason, both the good and the bad.

So given how much I adore it and how much meaning I found in it, why would I allow myself to doubt the awesomeness of *Star Wars*? Mostly because no matter how many times or in how many ways I try to interest my smart, wise, Gen Y sister in it, she persists in finding it dull, depressing, and "unmagical" (her word—by way of contrasting it with her generation's standard for magic, *Harry Potter*). She finds the characters unconvincing, the dialogue stiff, and the world lame—it's devoid, for her, of that spark that makes great science fiction or fantasy spring to life.

She's not alone here. Pauline Kael pretty much agreed with her. She wrote that "*Star Wars* is like getting a box of Cracker Jack which is all prizes"—all fluff, no substance (if candy-coated popcorn can function metaphorically as substance). She called it an "epic without a dream" with "no lyricism" and an "absence of wonder." And I guess I imagine, sometimes, what might happen if I were watching it now for the first time. I wonder if I might see more wooden dialogue and thematic vagueness and ham-fisted silliness. I wonder, in short, if I might not think it was that great.

And then I push those feelings deep down inside (another Gen X specialty) and go back to being spirited away by the brilliance and beauty of these movies. How do I pull that off? Well, to quote Yoda: *My ally is the Force, and a powerful ally it is.* Part of loving anything or anyone is not knowing exactly why.

And so no reasoned argument can change the way the opening blare of John Williams's score makes my hairs stand on end and my insides leap with anticipation. Nothing can dim the poignancy of Luke's heart-wrenching quest for a father figure, one that sends him to the doorsteps of a grumpy uncle, an old hermit, a green-skinned 900-year-old homunculus, and of course, the galaxy's reigning overlord of evil, only to rescue every single one of them from their otherwise lonely, childless existences and restore order to the galaxy in the process. Nothing Pauline Kael says can make me unfeel the horror of Obi-Wan's sacrifice or the tragedy of Alderaan's demise. No critique can dim the charm of Han Solo, whose debts hang over his head like so many unpaid parking tickets and who is rescued from his own half-hearted cynicism not by the Force but by friendship. In short, nothing anyone could ever say could convince me there isn't lyricism and wonder and magic in these movies.

Or for that matter, that they don't totally kick Harry Potter's ass.

USING *STAR WARS* IN REAL LIFE

Unlike algebra, the *Star Wars Trilogy* is fun and useful. Here's a guide
to employing some of the series' choicest quotes in common situations.

real-life situation	*star wars response*
Your buddy's looking for two people to buy his tickets to the John Mayer concert. Are you interested?	"These aren't the droids you're looking for."
The ice queen you've been dating for six months finally tells you she loves you.	"I know."
You're losing a game of ping-pong to an unusually talented eleven-year-old.	"The force is strong with this one."
Your friend says he's really busy but he'll try to pick you up at the airport tomorrow.	"Do or do not. There is no try."
Your six-year-old nephew dresses as an Imperial Stormtrooper for Halloween.	"Aren't you a little short for a Stormtrooper?"
You're really close to getting the high score on Guitar Hero.	"Almost . . . there . . ."
You've signed on to sell cosmetics/herbal supplements/financial services as part of a pyramid scheme.	"This deal is getting worse all the time."

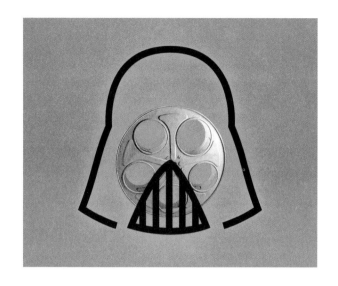

STAR WARS VS. TITANIC

TITANIC: HOOK, LINE, AND SINKER

 Have you ever listened to "My Heart Will Go On"? On repeat? For two hours straight? How about watched *Titanic* in the theater? Seven times? OK, fine, eight.

If you happen to have two X chromosomes and were born in the mid-eighties, chances are: yes. For any other human being, going through the aforementioned scenarios would, in theory, induce insanity. It would seem, however, that Gen Y girls are possessed of a certain gene that predisposed them to have a surprisingly high tolerance for Celtic pan flute music and iceberg-related disasters. Which is why *Titanic* had such a profound effect on us.

While I'm sure James Cameron is well aware that his three-hour-and-fourteen-minute melodrama created an enormous base of girl fans, I'm not sure to what extent he actually understands the degree to which *Titanic* completely took over our realities and monopolized our headspace. (He can't; he's a boy.) Following *Titanic*'s release, we transformed into an army of teen zombies. (So just in case you were worried about any impending zombie apocalypse, you can chill out, because it already happened in 1997.)

There's no disputing *Titanic*'s hugeness. The film occupied the number-one box-office spot for fifteen consecutive weeks; swept in the awards, taking home eleven Oscars; created one of the best-selling soundtracks; and made an estimated worldwide gross of some $2 billion. Which, until recently, made *Titanic* the highest-grossing film of all time, until *Avatar* unseated it in 2009. I feel this *has* to be a mistake. The fact that a movie featuring characters who look like descendants of the Blue Man Group just back from vacation in Montego Bay and a backdrop resembling the CG version of *FernGully*—I can't *even*.

But I'll forgive Cameron my bewilderment over *Avatar* for managing to concoct the most perfect spell with *Titanic*, one with thoughtfully balanced elements.

For starters, *Titanic* owes the majority—roughly 43 percent, by my calculations—of its amazingness to Leonardo DiCaprio, the undisputed heartthrob of the late nineties. The timing for Leo's casting as Kate Winslet's heroic love interest couldn't have been better. Just the year before, we'd flocked to the theaters to see the blond-locked actor play Romeo to Claire

Danes's Juliet. Baz Luhrmann's reprise of Shakespeare's most epic love story won us over with an interpretation that gave the drama modern, recognizable images. Sort of like a dystopian disco-glam episode of *Laguna Beach*. As far as we were concerned, Leo *was* Romeo; he *was* Jack Dawson. He was the most perfect boyfriend who would do things like chase you around a fish tank or hold your face in his hands while talking seriously. Or, you know, die for you. NBD.

Those familiar with Cameron know the man has a bit of an obsession with the shipwrecks and mysteries of the deep sea (see *The Abyss* and his record-setting solo submersible dives), so it's safe to assume that his inspiration for *Titanic* stemmed from his own sea-centric interests. However, as far as historical subject matter goes, he did well in choosing an event that wouldn't alienate Gen Y audiences. The myth of the *Titanic* was still well alive in the nineties, probably because it involved rich people (who ever gets tired of *those* sad losers?). Also, in elementary school music class, we were still singing that upbeat song "It Was Sad When That Great Ship Went Down," whose lyrics went "Husbands and their wives, little children lost their lives," although you probably remember the immensely more mature fifth-grader variation: "Uncles and aunts, little children lost their pants!"

Titanic may have been conceived as a Hollywoodized period piece, but to my romantic and naive mind, this was a window onto the past. "The past," as a topic in general, was something I was obsessed with as a kid. It started with a love for fifties poodle skirts and diners, and I only regressed further. I had a subscription to *Victoria* magazine and would tear out stories on "colonial farmhouse retreats" or photos of models dressed like adult American Girl dolls. Also, one Chanukah I asked for a wood hoop—a game in which you'd roll a wooden hoop along by tapping it with a peg—which was last popular in . . . 1898. I'll be the first to admit all of this is pretty weird. But for once, my friends seemed to be into it, too.

Titanic was a bonding movie. At a time when raging hormones basically made every day seem like the end of the world, it somehow seemed totally logical to repeatedly give our hard-earned allowances to Loews. For only six or so dollars, you could buy a cathartic experience. You'd simultaneously comprehend total loss, maintain hope for true love, and cry your eyes out with your girlfriends—which is all actually really fun. But after the first few viewings, you could move past the gut-wrenching shock, and then *Titanic* became a movie you could also see with boys because of (a) Kate Winslet's boobs and (b) massive destruction. It was to Jack and Rose's "I'm flying!" moment that I experienced my first sweaty hand-holding session. Nothing could have been more romantic.

Nothing, that is, except for slow dancing to Celine singing "My Heart Will Go On." That song, and the rest of the *Titanic* soundtrack, was in constant rotation at dances, on the radio, and in bedroom boom boxes between 1997 and 1998. All of the eighth-grade girls taking piano lessons at that time learned how to play "My Heart Will Go On," and we'd fight over the school piano in between classes to see who could play it with the most intensity.

To be fair, I should admit that I don't love *Titanic* the way I did back then (I think most people don't). Which is probably a good thing because otherwise I'd still be planning my wedding aboard the *Queen Mary* and cueing up Celine for my first dance. That dream sank long ago.

TITANIC

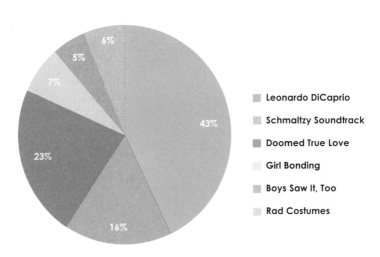

- Leonardo DiCaprio
- Schmaltzy Soundtrack
- Doomed True Love
- Girl Bonding
- Boys Saw It, Too
- Rad Costumes

GIRLS ON FILM

There was a moment when I realized boys truly sucked. Explaining my path to enlightenment would be a fruitless exercise, as one's arrival at this frame of mind tends to manifest without much logic. (Although the male-suckage paradigm tends to prove true.) The only tangible evidence I can give you would be the horror I felt at six years old when my mother came home from the video store with *An American Tail: Fievel Goes West*. A movie about a mouse who was a *boy*? I didn't want to see some dude adventure his way to victory for an hour and a half. What did this woman take me for? The pink Power Ranger?

When it came to movies, the ones that really interested me, from the time I was a young girl up until my tweenage years, were those with female leads who could offer me something in the way of daydream fodder—a cool bedroom, a boyfriend, a secret, or a magical power. As a result, my identity owes a part of its construct to a number of cinema girls with whom Gen Y had the opportunity to hang. Here are some of those ladies—who they were, what they taught us, and what they said about Gen Y:

DISNEY PRINCESSES

While several of the Disney princesses are generation-neutral, there's no denying how central these classic characters were to Millennials growing up. Nothing ever felt dated about Snow White, Sleeping Beauty, or Cinderella. In the nineties, Disney made a push to create stronger female role models who weren't just love starved and slender waisted. It did this by making characters "smarter": There was Ariel, the mer-nerd of *The Little Mermaid* and *Beauty and the Beast*'s "bookish" Belle. Or by giving them ethnicities other than, uh, white. There was a brief moment—probably around the time when I considered becoming a women's studies major and was really into Ani DiFranco and Tibetan prayer flags—when I would have argued that Disney princesses were fascist, heteronormative works of Satan. But seeing as I was a child who adored Disney princesses, I appear to have emerged from childhood relatively unscathed. I say Cinderella and the gang can relax and do their thing: provide endless hours of dress-up play and introduce the masses to classic stories.

LONELY GIRLS

What is it about orphans, and why do we get off on them? (If you took this last sentence literally: Please seek help.) During the early nineties, the girls we came across on film came from supremely fucked-up families. But even I'll admit there was something delicious about those scenarios. Consider the motherless characters like the death-obsessed Vada Sultenfuss from *My Girl* or *Casper*'s Kat Harvey as portrayed by Christina Ricci. In the eighties Jim Henson film *Labyrinth* (which performed abysmally in the box office but garnered a cult following with Gen Y on VHS), we meet Sarah, a teen plagued by a father and evil stepmother who make her always take care of her baby brother. Watch this movie now and you'll find Sarah to be a whiny cos-play nerd who would probably LiveJournal the crap out of her so-called dramatic life, but back then, her family seemed so horrible that it felt totally justifiable when Sarah wills her baby brother to be taken away by the Goblin King (as portrayed by a vain, legging-clad David Bowie, and yeah, you can totally see his thing through his pants).

POTENTIAL BFFS

Their characters aside, we also followed the lives of certain teen stars with fascination. I'm not ashamed to say that I honestly believed that I would one day be best friends with Lindsay Lohan, the Olsen twins, Michelle Trachtenberg, and Amanda Bynes. We were all going to drive around in convertibles and order banana splits with a spoon for each of us. On film, these girls were pristine portrayals of young Americans, and offscreen, they seemed like cool kids who could have grown up in your neighborhood. Never mind that most of them would end up going off the rails thanks to drugs, legal problems, eating disorders, or apparent insanity (see: Amanda Bynes, circa 2012). Still, there remained (and kind of still does remain) something relatable about these women that made us feel like our fantasies actually had some small basis in reality. LiLo, if you're reading: I'll always love you. No matter how batshit insane you are. MK & A: Call me.

GIRLS AS THE ROOT OF ALL EVIL

As much as we loved being girls, we also came to see that our own kind was often pitted against us in a sort of estrogen-charged civil war. The nineties

STAR WARS IV, V, VI
RAIDERS OF THE LOST ARK
E.T. THE EXTRA TERRESTRIAL
CADDYSHACK
FLETCH
ANNIE HALL
DO THE RIGHT THING
PURPLE RAIN
WHEN HARRY MET SALLY
FAST TIMES AT RIDGEMONT HIGH
VALLEY GIRL
SIXTEEN CANDLES
THE BREAKFAST CLUB
HEATHERS
SWINGERS
TRADING PLACES

DIRTY DANCING
THE PRINCESS BRIDE
LITTLE DARLINGS
A FISH CALLED WANDA
THE MUPPET MOVIE
MY OWN PRIVATE IDAHO
MIDNIGHT RUN
ANIMAL HOUSE
WAR GAMES
SAY ANYTHING
SID & NANCY
METROPOLITAN
PULP FICTION
SLACKER
BEING JOHN MALKOVICH

GEN Y DVDS

AMERICAN PIE
CAN'T HARDLY WAIT
CRUEL INTENTIONS
SCREAM
SHE'S ALL THAT
ROMEO + JULIET
EVER AFTER
THE CRAFT
GARDEN STATE
LOST IN TRANSLATION
CLUELESS
NAPOLEON DYNAMITE

MEAN GIRLS
TITANIC
JAWBREAKER
10 THINGS I HATE ABOUT YOU
HOME ALONE
A LITTLE PRINCESS
MY GIRL
NOW AND THEN
NEVER BEEN KISSED
PLEASANTVILLE
BLAIR WITCH PROJECT
LABYRINTH
BEAUTY AND THE BEAST
JUNO
CRAZY/BEAUTIFUL
I KNOW WHAT YOU DID LAST SUMMER

and early 2000s on film often showed us that; at best, girls could be your frenemies, and at worst, they could be psychotic Wiccans plotting your own suicide. And yet, sometimes these chicks could be grossly inspiring, like those weirdos from *The Craft* or Wednesday Addams, who took emo-goth to a whole new level. When it comes to the bullying epidemic we speak of in high schools, now we can look to *Mean Girls* and *Cruel Intentions* as precursory evidence—except these stories were awesome because they involved Lindsay Lohan, Manhattan private school junkies, and "Bitter Sweet Symphony."

LOVE CHASERS

Nothing gets straight to the heart of a teenage girl faster than Leonardo Di-Caprio's steely gaze. Coupled with the right leading lady you'd have imaginary makeout sessions for months, if not years, if not . . . decades . . . not like I still think about that stuff. Whatever. But star-crossed or wronged lovers would always be a point of obsession, whether it was in the Leo and Claire Danes remake of *Romeo + Juliet* or with *Titanic*'s Jack and Rose. And of course, may we never forget Drew Barrymore as a "real-life" Cinderella in *Ever After*, who not only came out on top but also caused a yearlong obsession with glitter eye gel, Renaissance-inspired hairstyles, and fairy wings as an everyday accessory. Not something easy to pull off with a JanSport backpack. Just sayin'.

THE SMARTER YOU ARE, THE MORE *CLUELESS* YOU GET

When *Clueless* came out in 1995, *Entertainment Weekly* critic Owen Gleiberman had this to say: "In the world according to Cher, Hamlet is that guy played by Mel Gibson, making love in a car is 'jeepin,' and a moment of anxious weirdness is summed up by the confession 'I'm having a *Twin Peaks* experience.'" To be clear, he said it like it was a *bad* thing. (He also devoted a whole creeptastic paragraph to Alicia Silverstone's "ripely precocious baby-doll allure.") He gave the film a C+, a grade Cher would have seen as a mere jumping-off point for negotiations but which the rest of us understood to be a clearly drawn battle line between those who get it and those who don't. (Also between those who unironically use the phrase "making love" and those who don't. But that's another essay.)

As an update of *Emma*, one of my favorite books ever, *Clueless* instantly became and remains my favorite Jane Austen adaptation, capturing all the entitlement, privilege, hubris, brattiness, unfulfilled potential, and mystifying likability of Emma Woodhouse in a thoroughly modern context, translating the charged dialogue between Emma and Knightley into pitch-perfect postmodern repartee. It seemed tailor-made for a latchkey generation weaned on MTV, eighties excess, and nineties irony, and the fact that it appeared to go over certain critics' heads just made us like it more—inconceivable though it was that someone could dislike it.

It was nearly as surprising to discover that just as many Millennials loved it as my friends and I did. Of course, when I think about it now, I see why: It's the story of Generation Y (Cher) falling in love with Generation X (Josh).

Think about it. Josh is a flannel-wearing, Nietzsche-reading, goatee-growing "loser" who listens to Radiohead, wants to practice environmental law, and dates surly girls in Doc Martens. According to Josh, Cher's a "superficial space cadet" who has no idea who Billie Holiday is, thinks classical architecture is something invented in the seventies, and yes, views grades as arbitrary measures of value to be manipulated by a good argument. Their clash is a mini-lesson in the gripes each generation has about the other (And arguably, a snapshot of the crisis of postmodern American life. But that's another essay).

We see their romance coming before they do, of course, because they're too busy sniping at each other, competing for the attention of the gruff father figure who calls his own parents "brain-dead lowlifes" but also insists that he divorces "wives, not children" when Cher complains that ex-stepbrother Josh isn't even a real relative. Josh disapproves of Cher's aggressive makeover of newcomer Tai, rightly accusing her of acting out her own mommy issues on the unsuspecting naïf; Cher sees through Josh's pretentious girlfriend's nattering and surprises her with a Mel Gibson–channeled command of *Hamlet* dialogue.

They resist, they fight, they wrestle—and then they give in to the realization that they need each other. Josh needs Cher's free-floating playfulness to help him laugh at himself; Cher needs Josh's earnestness to give her direction toward somewhere other than the mall; they both acknowledge that neither is really as clueless as they've made each other out to be. For them, as for all of us, the compromise that comes with loving someone different is what saves us from ourselves. When they get together in the end, suddenly the whole world just makes sense.

Which is, of course, what a great romance does: not just tell a story about two people getting together but a story in which that union represents some greater, more important order in the universe. The pleasure of *Clueless* is manifold: It's a contemporary commentary on the Austen-era romance, but it's a damn good example of it, too, giving as much traditional satisfaction as the pre-Victorian book it was based on. So Cher can pretend all she likes that the reason she wants to catch the bouquet at the end is to win $200. The rest of us know the truth, and it goes a little like this: As *if*.

HOW CHER HOROWITZ BECAME GEN Y'S BFF

 1997 was a big year for me: I learned leg hair was a scourge to be eradicated at all costs, Jockey training bras were the bomb, and *Clueless* was the greatest movie ever.

I was twelve, suddenly surrounded in a girl's world of my own creation with a fourteen-piece Lip Smackers collection, a stack of Hello Kitty notebooks, and a Leo DiCaprio closet collage/shrine. It was a stark contrast to whoever I'd been before, and the night someone popped *Clueless* into the VHS at a slumber party, Cher Horowitz managed to validate my entire existence. *Clueless* became my baseline barometer for cool and my guide to aspirational living—and, I'm not ashamed to admit, has remained deeply central to my life ever since.

Back then, I missed the note of satire; all I knew was Cher had a cell phone and a whole computer-controlled room for a closet. (A whole *room*, people.) And that was enough. Cropped sweaters and knee socks colonized our wardrobes. My friends and I learned to walk and talk like Cher, putting our thumbs together in W signs to our parents' faces. *Surfin' the crimson wave! Full-on Monet! Where's my white collarless shirt from Fred Segal?* Did we have any idea what any of this meant? As if.

It pains me to acknowledge an uncomfortable fact about my early relationship with *Clueless*, which is that I occasionally watched *Clueless*…

the TV show, which was on the air between 1996 and 1999. It may be the worst show of all time. If you want to torture someone, lock them in a room with this cheesy sitcom where the characters are seemingly doing whip-its and shopping at Fashion Bug; they will lose it.

The unsettling truth about *Clueless* the TV version is that it was dumbed down for people like me—young teenagers of the late nineties—who were too dumb/not yet worthy of relishing movie-*Clueless*'s poetic gems.

I like to think that, in my semiserious quest in becoming a full-time Cluelessologist, the TV version left me unscathed. Because as I got older, the original *Clueless* continued to yield rewards. Like a Bloomin Onion, it revealed deeper layers of comedy, commentary, and complexity with each viewing. This movie would tell me that Billie Holiday was not a man; that famous quotes came from Shakespeare, not CliffsNotes; and that "jeepin'" was not, strictly speaking, an extreme back-roading sport.

I won't tell you how many times I've seen *Clueless*, but I will tell you it's enough that I can pretty much recite the entire thing from memory. Sometimes when I can't sleep, I play the movie in my head, fast-forwarding through the scenes, testing my knowledge of the film's sequence.

The gift of *Clueless* kept on giving all through college, where I devoted term papers and impassioned speeches to the defense and dissection of *Clueless* as a seminal cultural document. You might even credit Cher and Co. with my choice to major in American Studies—home to film-school rejects and vinyl-clutching radio station denizens—where I acquired such real-world skills as waxing semiotic on the significance of Chuck Taylors and reality TV. And like Cher and her prototype Emma before her, I eventually learned that the joke was on me when I tried to find gainful employment armed with this dubious skill set.

What makes director Amy Heckerling's masterpiece so remarkable is that it grew up with me and never lost relevance. There aren't many things you embrace at age twelve that will continue to entertain and enchant for all sorts of equally valid, totally new reasons at sixteen, and twenty-one, and twenty-six. And while I did, at some point, have to come to terms with the fact that plaid schoolgirl suits never were and will probably never be an acceptable form of dress, I never lost my affection for Cher's sartorial bravado. And in all other areas, she remained untouchable as an icon of cool. Because while my appreciation for the movie deepened over time to include a smug grasp of the pop-cultural pastiche and postmodern shtick of it all, I never lost my original pleasure in the simple story of a girl who thinks she can control everything and learns that the world is full of surprises.

KING OF THE DIPSHITS: JOHN HUGHES, GEN X, AND THE GENIUS OF ANTHONY MICHAEL HALL

"It's really human of you to listen to all my bullshit."
—SAMANTHA, *SIXTEEN CANDLES*

 One evening a couple of years ago at the Los Angeles County Museum of Art, director Jason Reitman held a live table reading of John Hughes's *The Breakfast Club*, featuring Patton Oswalt as the geek, James Van Der Beek as the jock, Jennifer Garner as the princess, Mindy Kaling as the basket case, and Aaron Paul as the criminal. You don't even need to have been there to know what a Gen X (and, I'd imagine, Gen Y) bonanza this was. The casting alone is a testament to the movie's influence: Many of these actors' (and their contemporaries') on- or offscreen personas owe some debt to the archetypes Hughes defined. And the script seems unusually well suited to this sort of staging: The movie itself was static and talky, especially for an entertainment directed at 1980s teenagers. It was basically an ensemble *My Dinner with André* for kids, which sounds possibly like the worst pitch for a movie ever. And yet it was amazingly, enduringly awesome and still inspires reenactment by some of today's best actors.

Hughes's influence is so fully recognized: Everything that could be said almost certainly had been by the time of his untimely death in 2009 (and anything we'd missed surely got written in *Vanity Fair* after that). He both portrayed and helped build our generation's identity; he was a major voice in our culture's ongoing conversation about the definition, description, and adulation of adolescence. He did for teenagers what Charles Schulz did for little kids: He portrayed our milieu as a complete world, a culture unto itself, a subverse that often operated alluringly and scarily outside the influence of adults and authority figures. But for all of that, the love stories he told weren't exactly revolutionary, or at least don't seem that way now: They mostly involved two white people battling classic socioeconomic polarities (rich/poor, popular/unpopular) to get up on each other. There were no interracial trysts, no gay couples, no interfaith liaisons. His aim was not to subvert but to legitimize the struggles, sorrows, and social pressures experienced by suburban American teenagers. He recognized that music was a huge part of this landscape; the new-wave soundtracks were characters in their own right, testifying to the tribulations and terrors of youth and young love.

What I find more interesting these days is the way Hughes treated one archetype in particular: the nerd. Looking past the headgear and floppy disk badinage, you can see something really human in his geeks, and one in particular: Anthony Michael Hall, whose performances in *Sixteen Candles*, *The Breakfast Club*, and *Weird Science* remain the consummate Geek Trilogy of the eighties. They were all variations on the same character: a social pariah who is both an observer and a participant, a scapegoat and a catalyst, a dreamer and a doer. What would likely have been a slide rule–wielding caricature in other movies became something much more interesting and human in the hands Hall, whose visceral, intelligent portrayals somehow managed to combine the slapstick and the brutally honest, painful self-consciousness and foolish bravado. Critics praised his performances as endearingly goofy or well-played physical comedy, but they missed the point. He made the characters real and honest and heartbreaking, full of the hectic spasms of desire and honor and delusions of grandeur and premonitions of failure. His jittery, half-heartedly overconfident Farmer Ted in *Sixteen Candles* is so painful to watch because it's so fucking real and so self-aware and so weirdly brave: He's not actually in the dark about his outsider status, and he's not misreading the social cues, he's trying his hardest *in spite of them*, courageously and foolishly taking the knocks that such attempts render inevitable. His status as King of the Dipshits is hard-won and constantly under attack, and it seems to demand these repeated humiliations—but as he seems to know, it's the best he's going to do, this year, at least.

The resurrection of that character in *The Breakfast Club* and *Weird Science* definitely feels like variations on the same basic tropes and tics, but with different backstories—and in the case of *The Breakfast Club*, a code that signals a new sort of status for the nerd as spokesperson. The voiceover at the end of *The Breakfast Club* is less the point than that he is the one who writes and reads it, telling the story of the whole group. Granted, he's the only one who doesn't end up paired off—a lonely, solitary figure (for the time being, at least), but one who's in good company with the heroes of westerns and samurai movies. At that moment, we Gen Xers got perhaps our first glimpse of the future, in which the Farmer Teds became empowered to tell not just their own stories but ours as a generation—though even Hughes might not have anticipated quite how celebrated the nerds of the world would become.

Any doubt about that must have been done away by that table reading. There are plenty of meaningful connections to be drawn among that group—Paul's Jesse Pinkman as the direct descendant of John Bender's intelligent heart-of-gold delinquent; Van Der Beek's squeaky-clean Dawson as the next generation of high-haired Hughesian MVPs—but none so apt or important as Patton Oswalt's inheritance and transformation of the Anthony Michael Hall mantle. Because of Hall, we get performers like Oswalt and Rainn Wilson—actors who embody the realized potential of Hall's tentative, terrified adolescent character, self-assured heroes of searingly smart, unapologetic uncoolness. They, like Hughes himself, have created an archetype that endures for every Gen Xer: He may be a geek, but he's anything but a loser.

But what we found out
is that each one of us is
a brain, and an athlete,
and a basket case, a
princess, and a criminal.

Does that answer your
question?

Sincerely Yours,

The Breakfast Club

TEEN COMEDIES: NEW DORK CITY

 In the years leading up to Y2K, many a teenage boy's third eye was actually a third ball—the Hacky Sack. And as Freddie Prinze Jr. taught us, given the right amounts of hotness and insecurity, these magical foot sacks could prove successful in both attracting a mate (well, maybe) and finding one's inner path to enlightenment.

I'm talking, of course, about one of the greatest—and supremely underappreciated—scenes in teen comedy history, from the 1999 classic *She's All That*. Working on a bet that popular guy Zack Siler (Prinze) can turn the school's art freak, Laney Boggs (Rachael Leigh Cook), into the prom queen, Zack goes to Laney's bizarro performance art showing, only to be yanked up on stage himself. Zack produces a Hacky Sack from his pocket and begins bouncing it while delivering an intense monologue:

> Hack-e-sack. Hack-e-sack. Bounce! Bounce! Gotta keep bouncin'.
> Can't let it drop. Never let it drop. C'mon, Zack. Everyone's watching.
> Expecting . . . Don't. Ever. Let it. Drop!

In case you didn't get the message, this is some deep, intense stuff; a window onto the complexities of the teenage soul, if you will. But it's the layers and context of the scenario—popular kid, removed from his popular-kid posse, doing the dork's dance and thriving at it—that perfectly epitomizes the philosophy that often dominated Gen Y's canon of teen comedies. Contrary to logic, our heroes weren't the "cool" kids. Meaning that Millennials grew up watching cinematic worlds in which nerds triumphed and even the "normal," popular kids had their own inner freak shows (whether they realized it or not).

Our teen movies set us up to willingly rebel against the A-group and side with the kooks. In *American Pie*, we loved Jim for getting with a model as much as we loved him for getting with a pie. In *Can't Hardly Wait*, the unlikely invisible guy got the impossibly beautiful girl. In *Never Been Kissed*, Drew Barrymore did her best to disguise her inner dork but ultimately gained acceptance because of it. Whether their idiosyncrasies were more subtle ("But you love Ladysmith Black Mambazo!" re: Lindsay Lohan's character in

X VS. Y
TEEN COMEDY CHEAT SHEET

X	Y
FAST TIMES AT RIDGEMONT HIGH Sex and humiliation under the umbrella of airhead Valley antics and peer pressure.	**AMERICAN PIE** Sex and humiliation with a ticking clock, and a resulting series of puerile pranks and tomfoolery involving webcams, pies, and parents.
PRETTY IN PINK Motherless child from "the wrong side of the tracks" with a "wacky" fashion sense wins over elitist popular boy by being her true self.	**SHE'S ALL THAT** Motherless child from the wrong side of the OC with a taste for weird art reforms the rich guy with overly gelled hair.
THE BREAKFAST CLUB Over the course of a day, an "unlikely" group of teens reveal the humanity behind their stereotypes and overcome the tyranny of high school.	**CAN'T HARDLY WAIT** Over the course of a night, the soulless or brain-dead get what's coming to them; the geeks and outsiders get the hot girl and become millionaires.
HEATHERS Outsider on the inside revenge plot gone wrong with scrunchies and bombs.	**MEAN GIRLS** Outsider on the inside revenge plot gone wrong with fake boobs and pink on Wednesdays.

Mean Girls) or milked for dramatic effect, à la *Napoleon Dynamite*, Gen Y's characters tended to be just . . . kind of weird.

Of course, the underdog is nothing new in teen comedy (or any story, really), but we have Gen X to thank for giving us the template (props to John Hughes). We consumed this established trope because it worked and entertained. Little matter that Hughes's high school scenarios were about as unlikely as making men's nail polish a thing.

Perhaps we loved these characters not so much for their outlandish conflicts but because we actually had shared goals and desires. If dreaming about being the most awesome kid in school while simultaneously having really bad acne or any other teenage impediment is part of the American experience, then we can identify with our protagonists. As for all the people who actually were at the top of the social ladder—all the homecoming queens and star quarterbacks—well, who were those freaks? You can only look back at them and think of them as such.

These movies would end up reflecting a certain truth about high school, which is that the stuff you remember is never "awesome." The stories you tell are the ones that illuminate your own stupidity. Like the time you thought smoking oregano was the same thing as smoking pot. Or when you decided it'd be a good idea to perform an interpretive dance for your tenth-grade *Hamlet* final. Or how you got into going to those sketchy improv-dance-jams. Or that time in ninth grade when you got really into vintage culottes. Or when, as a freshman, you worked up the courage to ask the prettiest senior girl for a cigarette, like no big deal, you totally smoke all the time, and when she offered a light, you simply extended the cigarette tip toward the lighter, a good two feet from your face. And when she told you that you had to inhale in order to get it lit, you said, "Well, that's how they do it in Europe. I went there. And they light them like that there."

But had you been with the in-crowd, you'd never have these stories to tell. And even if you were a Josie Grossie, at least you weren't the girl who'd called you that in the first place. Even if she was really, really pretty.

COMMODORE 64

NAPSTER

**PALM
PILOT**

APPLE

DISCMAN

AOL

ATARI

SIDEKICK

WALKMAN

CDS

AIM

BETAMAX

TAMAGOTCHI

CHAPTER 6

TECHNOLOGY

———————

X INTRO

RAGE AGAINST THE MACHINE

 Ah, technology. From the Greek *techno* meaning "electronic music" and *logy* meaning "log-like," we get the term that means "something you didn't know you needed but now can't imagine living without, like a log or electronic music."

I have this theory that ten thousand years from now, humans of the future will go looking for archeological relics from *one* thousand years from now, and all they will find is a single device the size of a postage stamp that does EVERYTHING—phone calls, photos, calendar, grocery shopping, laundry, child rearing, math, grant writing, massage therapy, movies, cooking, spell-check, weather forecasts, nose-hair trimming, relationship counseling, time telling, music playing, music making, breath freshening, and, naturally, social networking. And they will simultaneously know everything and nothing about the people who invented and used these things.

That I won't live to see this incredible advance doesn't bother me. If anything, I feel as if I've seen too much already. My relationship to technology, as for many of my generation, is confused and contradictory. Generation X undoubtedly has a thirst for the new, a lust for the latest. But we also have a rapacious nostalgia that extends to the relics of our youth, which is why you'll often see a turntable and an analog phone and a Super 8 camera and a Gutenberg-era printing press in an Xer's home. We, like those before us, have resisted the notion that the tools of our heyday are obsolete; we have insisted against all reason and evidence that vinyl just sounds better and landlines are more private, aware though we may be that we sound suspiciously like those stupid people who dismissed the first talkies as a passing fad and telephones as toys. You can't really blame us; we come from the past, after all, a time when a "library" was an actual place, not a bunch of files on your hard drive.

Yet we're not blindly nostalgic, or at least not in an acquisitive way. We draw the line at a great deal of obsolete technology, including Walkmans, Palm Pilots, and VCRs, after all. At least part of our interest in gadgets old and new is linked to our obsession with quality and authenticity, and to the suitability of the form to the function. No one has ever made the argument that the sound quality of a cassette tape is better than a CD, and everyone agrees that where portability is concerned, you can't do much better than an iPod. (YET.)

Moreover, the things we tend to cling to the most are the ones that went beyond their function to become rituals of sorts: Pulling out a record, cleaning it with that fuzzy little cylindrical brush, placing it gently on the turntable—it's all part of the experience, one that gets lost in the point-and-click upgrade of digital. We miss, at times, the sheer *there*ness of our old technology—the physical effort it takes to hit a typewriter key or dial a phone makes us feel grounded, attached, tied to the act in a way that gets lost with the touch technology of tablets and the masslessness of mp3 files. We Xers like artifacts, things, objects, collectibles—and a "library" of digital files just doesn't impart the same sense of accomplishment as a shelf full of books or LPs. In our childhood and adolescence, medium and message reinforced each other, became fused together, slobbered their meaning all over each other, until it wasn't just the song itself we loved but the thing it was recorded on, the cover for that thing, the shelf we stored it on, and the room where that shelf was. (Yes. I'm talking about my husband's "record room.") We attached our love to actual things, things which had a distinct and differentiated purpose: The idea that your phone is also your camera is also your record player is also your TV is not one that, at first anyway, was calculated to please us. We liked our stuff, our specialized devices, our possessions whose forms bespoke their function.

Which isn't to say we're Luddites. No, if anything, we're just fetishists in both directions, loving the old and the new, the past and the future simultaneously. When it comes to wanting the absolute latest, newest, shiniest toy, we're as guilty as the next guy in line at the Apple Store—guiltier, as recent statistics have begun to reveal. So how do we reconcile this inner conflict? How do we choose? Well, we don't. We just BUY EVERYTHING. And back to our obsession with quality, we make sure that we have "the best" in both categories, old and new. The best Technics SL-120 turntable from the seventies, the best speakers, the best plasma TV, the best MacBook, the best vintage Smith Corona typewriter, the original vinyl and the digitally remastered version. Only then can our restless, searching hearts rest in the hope that somewhere, among all that fucking stuff, there awaits the perfect, connoisseur-worthy experience.

But we're a dying breed, or certainly will be in a thousand years. By the time the humans of ten thousand years from now start digging, our collections will have been extinct for too many centuries to have left a trace, and in their place will be only the aforementioned iEverything. Those future humans will marvel at it, no doubt, and study its properties, and wonder why their ancestors persisted in calling it a "smart phone" when it always seemed to drop calls, and there won't be a single Gen Xer anywhere to talk up his trusty old Cortelco 2500 desk phone, and the world may actually be poorer for it. Or not.

Y INTRO

AMERICA: TECH YEAH!

Y Log in to AOL in the early nineties, and there wasn't much to see. Just a page of buttons for things like "Sports," "Today's News," "People Connection," or "Computing," which just makes no sense to me now because aren't you already on the computer? But there was also a section for AOL's younger users, called "Kids Only." The biggest draw in this section was the chat rooms, and there were three types of people you'd meet there:

1. Boys (one can only hope) looking for online girlfriends.
2. Braggers who talked only of horses or dirt bikes.
3. Girls who stirred up drama for attention.

This was the late nineties, a time when one could still be semi-anonymous online, defined only by a/s/l, the font and color of your typings, and possibly some type of avatar. No personal photos. No Google results should you let your real name slip and forget that you already told everyone you're "Jasmine LaFonte."

Kids Only wasn't exactly a friendly space. Inevitably, you'd log in to find yourself in the middle of a confusing transcript that was largely an ALL CAPS fight. I remember the time I logged in to meet MARY QUEEN OF DARKNESS, who had a goth-looking icon of a cloaked witch. Mary Queen of Darkness was going on about how her sister had died that day in a car accident. This wasn't going over very well with much of the crowd, who said "ur lying" or "if she died then ud b at her funeral." I felt bad for Mary so I rushed to her defense and angrily told those scrubs to back off. Mary thanked me, and I felt good about having stuck up for a stranger. Thing was, the next day, Mary Queen of Darkness logged in and announced to the group that she was sad because her sister had died today. Um, no. You said she died *yesterday*.

This made me realize that it was easy enough to be anyone online, and so I spent my early days on the Web inventing personalities in AOL chat rooms. There wasn't a lot else to do online. They'd told us about the World Wide Web in school (always with accompanying spiderweb drawings). The way our teachers described it, the rest of the Internet sounded like a boring library trip.

But true obsession with dial-up (much to my parents' annoyance) came once instant messenger and e-mail became available as a mode for sub-stituting phone conversations with people I already spent eight hours a day with. This became very, very important. I found I had learned a certain boldness and style that allowed me to show a different side of myself to the rest of my middle school peers. I changed e-mail addresses frequently; it was like opting for a new style, much in the way I tended to experiment with Clairol semiper-manent hair dye. One month, I was Medium Champagne Blonde and x-girl@gurlmail.com. The next, Auburn Spiced Tea and PrincessPear224@hotmail.com. IM let us gossip—unfiltered—catalyzing the time it took to make and break alliances or ask out/dump the object of your affection.

This was what we understood the Web to be—one giant phone con-versation. But of course the dot-com boom turned it into so much more than that, and as things advanced, our adoption of all things digital felt completely natural. Although Gen Xers and even boomers were the ones creating the technologies we grew up on, by the time we came into young adulthood, we'd started our takeover. We dominated MySpace with oversized sunglassed portraits, aired laundry on LiveJournal, blogged, Tweeted, Facebooked, downloaded, commented, shared.

All of this has led us to a place where people think of us as oversharers, and for some, that's true. You have your young parents who feel compelled to update the world on their baby's bowel movements or your girls who blog way too much about their sad single lives (even I'm guilty of this one). But somewhere along the line, all of this putting yourself out there became the norm. I have no issue expressing myself through the various social media channels I'm on: Tumblr, Twitter, Facebook, Instagram, Spotify, the list goes on. One of my favorites these days is Pinterest, the female-centric photo-sharing site that's had its fair share of feminist critique that women are using it to promote thinspiration and outdated housewife ideals. To me, quite the contrary: Here's a place where I can finally gather photos of my dream life and not feel shame about it. Do I acknowledge the slight lameness in spending an evening drinking wine and Pinning photos of mason-jar DIY projects? Sure, but I don't feel bad about people knowing. And yes, I may have a Pinterest board for all the world to see titled "Single Girl with a Wedding Pinterest Board/Leo's Wedding Fall 2016." My credo? If you Pin it, he will come.

Eve, however, feels a distinct discomfort and sense of confusion when it comes to using social media. And it's true: The times she's Tweeted or blogged, it just hasn't felt right, but I can't quite explain why. (Sorry.) She says it's because, unlike me, she didn't construct an online identity concurrently with an IRL one. And that might be true, because Gen Yers don't even like to think of having two different identities, despite the fact that you may feel Google has a very different idea of who you are and that others' perception of your digital you isn't always the truth.

Yet it's hard to deny how insanely emotional and real online activity can be. The love you can feel from 103 "happy birthday" Facebook posts. The betrayal when you catch a boyfriend receiving a blow job from a stranger in Second Life. I once fell for a Dutch man I met through Tumblr and whom I eventually got to know through Gchat and Skype. This relationship is one of my most haunting ones because our real lives could never coexist. And even *we* realized that continuing a love affair online would be supremely fucked up. And so I had to let that person go completely.

But the fact that any of this can happen now is amazing. We feel we can have a voice, and we use it both to rebel (see: commenting wars) and unite (see: getting the forty-fourth president of the United States elected, fuck yeah). What's more, Millennials are passionate about finding new inventions and uses, so many of us pour all our hopes into start-up sites and apps. Yes, it may look somewhat stupid to think that your social couponing–cum–music platform app is your ticket to the good life. But for Gen Y, technology is our new American dream. And no one can blame Americans for being eternal optimists. We all had to learn it somewhere.

Every Device You Owned

KAYPRO

CASETTE TAPE

EARLY MACINTOSH COMPUTER

WALKMAN

FLIP PHONE

PALM PILOT

CDS

NOKIA CELL PHONE

GAME BOY

BEEPER

TURNTABLE

IBOOK

IPOD

TAMAGOTCHI

NINTENDO

BOOMBOX

so when you were in college.
how did you write your papers?

 well first i had this computer called a KAYPRO

in high school did you write on computers

 no

on a typewriter i guess

oh god

 yeah it was a nightmare

that must've been the WORST

 i mean, sort of. like now it seems like it.
but back then we were like "omg can you
imagine having to WRITE THIS BY HAND"

and you did all your research...from...books?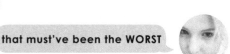

 yes books from the library

a library is a place full of books

or used to be

o

i went there once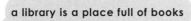

 are you sure it wasn't a bar called "the library"

too drunk to remember

 but yeah doing research was the worst. and even in my first magazine job u had to go to the library for stuff
but yeah doing research was the worst. and even in my first magazine job u had to go to the library for stuff

dude

 like finding old articles about people and all that. and for fact-checking we had a bunch of reference books

and then even when the internet came around, it was fuckin useless at first

 i know

but now nobody cares if something is accurate so it matters less

that's not truuuue

 but yeah it was way more of a pain in the ass to do anything. but we didn't know it

like nowadays people sometimes talk about how great it will be when they can teleport places, but not that much. mostly they're just really psyched about their cars

you know what's going to be weird? when in like 100 years, people are reading old Tumblrs (assuming they're still around) as, like, original sources. artifacts of a century ago

 yes they will be the encyclopedia britannica of the future

i am definitely planning on leaving mine for my daughter. so she can learn from the mistakes of my early 20s.

 i'm sure they'll treasure it. i guess i will leave my facebook feed. since i don't have a tumblr

you should tweet more

 it's so hard

what are you talking about. it takes like 2 seconds and you just push a button. boom. tweeted. done.

 also i have like 11 followers

you need to tweet to get followers

 too much pressure. i want followers first

ok, that's NOT greedy

 well mostly i don't really care. although i like that instagram. i'm getting more into that

it took u a while though

 yeah

i'm a surly adopter

Although if you're a high school dropout who has just sold his Internet company for $5 million, you apparently don't have to learn anything at all.

TEMPTATION, FRUSTRATION: GEN X AND APPLE

Once upon a time, someone named Eve (not me) got talked into trying an apple. You could call this the first instance of peer pressure—*Dude, don't you want to be cool, like God?*—and like most peer pressure, it was duly passed on to the next schlub via pretty much the same tactics. We all know how that ended: Thanks to those two, the rest of us have to toil in misery under the threat of eternal damnation (rats!) while wearing clothes (not so bad!) and knowing the difference between good and evil (kind of?).

A few years later, at Williams College, someone named Eve (me) was also—wait for it—seduced by an Apple.

My first computer, the one I arrived at college with, was a Kaypro. I know. That sounds like a fake name for a fictional technology company run by evil dorks, but it was unfortunately a real thing, a thing that looked like a computer from an eighties TV show about a sixties movie about the future, a painted metal-and-plastic thing that took up a whole desk and made embarrassing *boop-be-blerp-boop* noises. My roommate teased me mercilessly about it until eventually I got an Apple IIe so I could be like everyone else.

This was, you understand, before cell phones, before e-mail, before the Internet. Oh, there were hints of such things to come, but they were vague, abstract concepts that most often got expressed as computer-animated 3-D "virtual reality" environments that looked like Dire Straits' "Money for Nothing" video. If the iPhone was a twinkle in Steve Jobs's eye, we couldn't see it. Computers had one purpose in our lives, and that was as word processors, an upgrade from the typewriter. And until Apple came along, we didn't think of them as objects of desire. They were more like hair dryers or blenders—means to an end, things you used and then didn't think about until the next time.

As personal computing caught on, there grew two factions: Windows/PCs vs. Apple. And again, most of us were never once in danger of pushing the limits of these machines' capacities. We e-mailed, we wrote stuff, we played solitaire, all tasks either type of machine was more than equipped to handle. What Apple gave us that Windows and PCs didn't was the absolute unity of hardware and software, aesthetics and operating system: The two were one, mirror reflections of each other, and in marrying the two, Apple gave us actual objects to lust after, not just functionality we needed. They created not just a computer but a brand, a user experience. From the beginning, their proposition to us was: *This is not something you use, it's something you are. It's not a tool, it's a lifestyle choice.* It spoke to us, but not in that computer monotone voice from the movies that glumly droned, "Greetings, respected user." Apple's persona, in my mind anyway, was of an adorable, highly intelligent creature, a cross between Stephen Hawking and Hello Kitty with a dash of R2-D2, who waved amiably and said stuff like "Hey there! I like you already!" They took the "personal" in personal computer seriously; they sought not just our patronage, not just our consumption, but our love and loyalty.

And they got it. Before Apple came along, my friends and I enjoyed rejecting the notion of "brand loyalty." We dismissed it as a late capitalist co-opting of the notion of freedom—one that forced us to attach ourselves to one corporate entity (e.g., Coke) or another (e.g., Pepsi) based on the illusion of choice. (Let me be clear: This "objection" in no way deterred my insane diet soda consumption over the last three decades.) But the truth about us turned out to be different. The truth was that the reason we rejected big consumer brand loyalty was that no one had yet created a big consumer brand just for us.

Anyway, back to me. Since relinquishing my Kaypro II, I've often bought and used Apple products, but never exclusively; I've been an intermittent iPhone user, with long and dramatic dalliances with my old flame/nemesis, BlackBerry. I have always been able to appreciate the Apple brand without necessarily being a user of it, which, far from making me a bad brand loyalist, might be the key to being a pretty good one. While certain devices seem absolutely perfect to me—the MacBook Air I'm typing this on, or an iPod—I can never get past the feeling that my iPhone is optimized not to be a phone or e-mail/ texting tool (my primary uses for it) but as a social media device and mp3 player. My iPad, which is delightful as an object, sits unused while my Kindle comes everywhere with me. My BlackBerry never dropped calls, and it was on the same carrier that iPhone users so often blame for those malfunctions. Yet when BlackBerry comes out with something new, I'm never very interested.

The point of brand loyalty, after all, is to forge a relationship with your customer that gets you past those bumps in the road; the odd product that fails on one level or another can be overlooked if there's enough love and trust to tide you over. And in turn, my infidelities with other technology brands are easily overlooked—the Apple user interface continues to be so seamless and easy that coming back always feels familiar, like picking up just where I left off. In short, while I don't always buy or end up liking every single one of Apple's products, I'm buying what they're selling in a bigger, more important way.

So I have no doubt that the next time Apple comes out with something I find truly covetable, it will only be a matter of time before I reach out and grab it. Temptation, I guess, is the one thing that doesn't change.

PLEASE DON'T TELL ANYONE I HATE MY IPAD

 Y Please don't tell anyone I hate my iPad. Please. I don't even want to admit this to myself, I'm so ashamed. You see, Gen Y doctrine expressly stipulates that any verbal assault, ill will, or ignorance toward Apple is punishable by imprisonment in a pair of too-tight skinny jeans for up to ten years (or the time it takes to wait in line for the porta-potties at Coachella, whichever is longer). I'd probably get off easy, considering I own an iPad 1—a first-generation hand-me-down from a generous relative—which greatly reduces the offense. But still, I doubt I'd be able to get one guy working the Genius Bar to flirt with me if he knew that all I'd ever used it for was to download the *Twilight* books. Which I then deleted. And downloaded again.

But in all other respects, I am a loyal, law-abiding follower. I'm perhaps not as devout as those disciples who camp outside Apple Stores on product release days. These people aren't limited to my generation, but we make up a large faction, and to us, the concept of a life without Apple is just . . . *Wait, why would you even SAY that?!*

Our hunger, our devotion: It's actually not our fault. Little did we know it, but Steve Jobs Zoolandered us, resetting our brains each time we heard that angelic and reassuring chord at the start-up of our computers.

It's embedded in us a feeling of pure necessity, which is what drives us to upgrade whenever possible: *Me need iPad Mini NOW!! iPad Mini good.*

This is also evidenced by our apparent need to own multiple objects that all essentially do the same thing, and to use them all at once. How else is one supposed to watch a movie, text, and read a recipe for kale chips without a MacBook, iPhone, iPod Touch, and iPad? In my opinion, this is all doable on one device—up until the point that I decide it's time to download *Twilight* again.

And in our ongoing love affair with irony, we'll even embrace Apple's dated technologies, namely the podcast, which has made a comeback among Millennial guys. I don't know when this happened, but all of a sudden every dude has a podcast, usually covering such fundamental topics such as veganism, erotic fanfiction, or comedy.

But the fact is, we're OK being programmed to live our lives this way because we've learned (thanks to Apple) that there are two types of people in the world: Macs and PCs. And the alternative just seems way less fun, possibly involving spreadsheets, dad-like dance moves, and the wearage of khaki Dockers and belt clips.

Some think we're addicted, too attached, and that we even treat our devices with the same emotional weight we give to humans. They're right. But why say it like it's a bad thing? Is it so wrong to inadvertently squeal each time your iPhone dings with an exciting text? Or to feel comfort in having something to occupy awkward friend-is-late-again moments? And while I sometimes think I'd prefer the empty space in my bed to be occupied by another human, my MacBook often makes a decent substitute, its soft, blinking sleep light matching my own breathing.

So while my feelings about the iPad may be ambivalent, I can proudly announce MacBook and I are in a wonderful, loving relationship. I love you, MacBook.

AN ODE TO GURL.COM, THE ORIGINAL GIRLS' CLUB

Teenage girls are the worst. I know this because I was one once. Aside from being melodramatic and positively uptight about getting a hundred hairbrush strokes in each night, these girls are mean. They'll call you a slut. They say "shut up" when you're not talking. They wear pink on Wednesdays.

And they're evil geniuses when it comes to cyber-warfare against their own kind. At least, this is how we evolved. But once upon a time—1996, to be precise—the queen bees were at peace, and their kingdom was called gURL.com.

Leading up to '96, the Internet was something of a wasteland for teen or tweenage girls. gURL changed all that, providing a cool online community where we could talk to one another and create our identities. And astonishingly, gURL members were *nice*. Really, really nice.

Back then, the site had an indie/DIY vibe that did girliness just right: It balanced style with real-world issues without being condescending. gURL's cofounders—Rebecca Odes, Heather McDonald, and Esther Drill—wanted to make up for the lack in frank teen content out there, making the site's mission about honesty and openness. Finally, here was a place that addressed all the real issues you were dealing with (sex stuff, parental stuff, friend stuff, WTF is happening to my body stuff) and made the experience of getting over them kind of fun. You had "Help Me Heather," a popular advice column; articles about cool ladies like Gertrude Stein and Patty Smyth; comics and illustrations; and games like Paper Doll Psychology or one where you had to pop pimples. And remember gURL Palace? A little virtual world where you could create your own avatar? That was sick.

But what really made gURL special was the bulletin boards, where we talked to each other about pretty much anything from the totally mundane (are ponytails cool?) to the life threatening (I just got dumped). Thanks also to gURL e-mail accounts and customizable Web pages, we felt a certain ownership over the site, so we worked hard to keep it a special space. Of course, our kingdom wasn't immune to attacks, but we had a skilled defense. As soon as someone dared step out of line in a forum or hated on another gURL, users would say, "That's not OK," and show a rush of support. We didn't have the power to excommunicate, but once haters saw they were unwelcome, you didn't hear much from them again. We didn't realize it at the time, but the fact that a group of teenage girls self-policed to maintain niceness? Amazing.

In 1998, dELiA*s bought gURL.com, and though that shifted the site's identity slightly, I still hung on as an active fan. But over the next few years, I'd fall out of touch with gURL, and the site would change ownership several times, inevitably morphing its image along the way. I guess this is to be expected; change happens and nothing can stay the same forever. This is a lesson we all have to learn. I learned mine at my favorite website: gURL.com.

GENERATION X

YM MAGAZINE

HIGH
FIDELITY

SASSY

THE
PERKS OF
BEING
A WALL-
FLOWER

INFINITE JEST

WEETZIE
BAT

GHOST
WORLD

JUDY BLUME

HARRY POTTER

SWEET
VALLEY HIGH

CHAPTER 7

BOOKS AND MAGAZINES

_____

X INTRO

PIG TALES: GEN X LIT AND CHARLOTTE'S WEB

 Where books are concerned, there is, naturally, a generally accepted list of titles closely associated with Generation X—written in our lifetimes for or by us, featuring subject matter that seems vaguely indigenous to our emotional and cultural terrain (yuppies, slackers, depressives, and the like). It includes books like *Generation X* (duh); *Infinite Jest*; *Where the Sidewalk Ends*; *High Fidelity*; *The Beauty Myth*; *Ghost World*; *The Secret History*; *A Heartbreaking Work of Staggering Genius*; *Less Than Zero*; *Bright Lights, Big City*; *The Corrections*; *Are You There God? It's Me, Margaret*; *Fight Club*; *Prozac Nation*; *The Virgin Suicides*; *Bridget Jones's Diary*; and the Encyclopedia Brown books. (This might not be exactly your list, but I bet your list has a bunch of stuff by the same authors or some of their friends.) I have read and loved a lot of these books, but for me, none of them will ever, ever live up to—or be more Gen X than—*Charlotte's Web*.

I'm aware that it was published in 1952 and that E. B. White was definitely not a member of my generation. But that's the thing about books; they're not like movies and TV shows, which bear the mark so plainly of their time and place of origin. People tend to claim a book as their own regardless of the date of publication, so that a Gen Xer like me may be just as likely to think of *The Little Prince* (published in 1943) or *Pride and Prejudice* (1813) as something that's mine as, say, *American Psycho* (which I've never read). I'm even loath to let my sister claim Harry Potter for her generation—*Awww, come on, my friends and I love those books!* More than with other storytelling mediums, a book only really comes to life when someone starts reading it—all the dialogue, the action, the imagery lives in your head. So while I do identify with many of the authors and books that are considered typical Gen X fare, I never felt restricted in any way to them. And the books I find myself bonding with peers over are often not on that list: the Chronicles of Narnia, *A Wrinkle in Time*, anything by Jane Austen, *The Lord of the Rings*, *The Hunger Games*, and all of E. B. White's children's books.

But there's something about *Charlotte's Web* in particular: It reads to me like a Gen X story. For one thing, it starts with the line "Where's

Papa going with that ax?"—totally badass. But where White really nails it is with the characters. Not the human ones, who cluster in quaint, fifties-era nuclear families and attend state fairs, but the animals at Zuckerman's barn, who form a sort of rural version of the urban family—a diverse, symbiotic, disenfranchised hodgepodge of odd little family units and lone singletons. If Orwell's *Animal Farm* presented the barnyard as the center stage of History with a capital "H," White gave us a barnyard as societal microcosm, with characters many of us Xers would grow up identifying with—especially Wilbur the pig and Charlotte the spider.

Wilbur (who I feel the need to point out was *not* breastfed) is exiled from his family of origin (he's like the porcine Luke Skywalker!) and proceeds to wander from surrogate mother to surrogate mother, alternately resenting and clinging to the confines of his life in the barn, feeling strangely special but awfully lonely, and obsessing over his own death. His childhood is first cut short when he's rejected by his mother and then prolonged by Fern, who feeds him with a bottle and pushes him around in a baby carriage. He reminds me of a precocious child, haunted by the specter of his own gruesome demise. In other words, any number of characters in a Spike Jonze or Wes Anderson movie.

And then, of course, there's Charlotte—the other half of the Gen X psyche. Cerebral and creative, motherly and literate, rational but loving: She is the person (spider) who represents the saving power of friendship, of words, of language. She is smarter than everyone in the room, gets how people think, and knows how to sell an idea. She's philosophical and unsentimental, Mark Darcy to Wilbur's bumbling but lovable Bridget Jones. "What's a life, anyway?" she asks from her deathbed at the fair. "We're born, we live a little, we die."

These, to me, are the two sides to the Gen X personality: on the one hand stunted, childlike, lonely, precocious but not grown up; on the other, smart, savvy, capable of critical thought and deep loyalty. And they came together as one of the oddest dynamic duos in literature to show us a model for friendship and mutual understanding and blended families in a place where spiders and little girls parent pigs and then pigs turn around and parent rats and little spiders.

As a story, *Charlotte's Web* also gave me friends during my own sometimes-lonesome childhood. White sums it up pretty well at the end: "It is not often that someone comes along who is a true friend and a good writer. Charlotte was both." I've been trying to live up to that standard my whole life.

Y INTRO

AMERICAN NOBILITY

Y When you attend a Manhattan private school, you miss out on a lot of things average American teenagers get as part of their normal high school experience. No big games or tailgate parties. No homecoming queens. No school dances, although we did have proms, which I remember feeling so inconsequential because they seemed to last for only an hour: People would make an appearance and duck out to the after-party to have sex and do drugs.

I was a weird kid who bounced around from group to group, which meant whatever weekend rituals went on, I wasn't a part of them. So I spent most of my Saturday nights at my local Barnes & Noble, hoping that some other teenaged nerd with the same proclivity would fall in love with me. We'd meet, of course, by reaching for the same copy of *Leaves of Grass* or *Romeo and Juliet*.

It was really a lot to ask of your local Barnes & Noble. And between you and me, it didn't live up.

But I loved it there. I wish I could say that instead of a cheesy megachain, it was some quaint, independent bookstore, but part of the B&N appeal was the accomplishment of fishing out a selection from an impossibly huge collection of books. And they had Frappuccinos there, too. Not only delicious, Frappuccinos also make you look cool.

This was where I spent most of my allowance. The thought of checking out books from a library didn't appeal to me. I wanted to own everything I read and to build up a library, so that when people would come over, they'd see how well read and smart I was, and think, *That Leonora Epstein is so well read and smart.* No one ever really came over. But if they did, they would have seen a wall filled with classics, trash, and everything in between—Martin Amis, Goosebumps books, Salinger, Sedaris, Plath, Tolstoy (actually, I've never read any Tolstoy, but making people *think* you've read Tolstoy seems like a good thing to do).

Not to bash on Generation Z, but I thank my lucky stars I went to high school and college during a time when IDS (Internet distraction syndrome) wasn't quite in full force; otherwise, I'm fairly certain my reading lists would have been completely eviscerated by David After Dentist or marathons of illegally downloaded *Friends* episodes. It pains me to imagine who I would be without that collection of books. One of the scariest things I've ever experienced—scarier than Fear Street #6: *The Dead Lifeguard*, more terrifying than Britney with no hair—is a video in which a toddler manipulates an e-book on an iPad with ease but can't figure out why nothing happens when she swipes her finger across the page of an *actual* magazine.

So, I'm now an old person who is nostalgic for my memories of reading (on real paper and all). This was a time when I could legitimately count reading as a hobby, as it was something I did for fun, even after getting through the hundreds upon hundreds of pages of Derrida required for my Intro to Lit Theory class, which should be enough to turn someone off to reading for good. I can recall certain moments of epic literary satisfaction—dipping my feet in a pool and devouring the latest *Harry Potter*; being drawn into the darkness of *Girl, Interrupted*; experiencing the magic of *Breakfast at Tiffany's*; thinking for one deranged moment that *Chicken Soup for the Teenage Soul* was a good book, realizing a week later that it was the worst.

It shames me to admit that reading these days is a challenge. It's a rare day when I can access the different headspace it requires to disappear into a book. I feel as though there is a physical place—a room—in my brain where this type of thinking happens, and every time I try to go there, I spend the majority of the time pushing on the door when it is so clearly labeled "pull." The few times in the recent past that I've flown through a book? *Twilight* and *The Hunger Games*.

But seriously, let's keep this little secret between us, because my OkCupid profile says I'm currently reading *Infinite Jest*. I should probably change that.

Oh, and P.S.: Thanks for reading this book. I like you.

X

GENERATION X

High Fidelity

GHOST WORLD

A Supposedly Fun Thing I'll Never Do Again

Prozac Nation

The Secret History

FIGHT CLUB

Bright Lights, Big City

THE Preppy Handbook

Y

Tuesdays with Morrie

Harry Potter

The Perks of Being a Wallflower

Ella Enchanted

PERSEPOLIS

Fear Street

The Virgin Suicides

PREP

THE Girl's Guide to Hunting and Fishing

GIRL, INTERRUPTED

THE ZINE IS DEAD. LONG LIVE THE ZINE!

 According to Wikipedia, the first zine may have been published in the late eighteenth century by none other than Benjamin Franklin, confirming my long-held suspicion that he actually invented everything in the whole world everywhere. It was a literary circular written by and for mental patients at Pennsylvania Hospital—which is to say, it probably had more readers than most zines.

A zine (a term generally considered to be a shortened form of "fanzine") is typically a self-published periodical with a small circulation, usually devoted to a single topic of cult or niche interest, most often produced on a photocopier. Zines had been around for a long time before their heyday in the 1990s, gaining a fair amount of popularity among the pulp sci-fi fan base of the 1930s and forties, also known as the top commenters of their day. But when most of us think of zine culture, we think of riot grrrls and grunge and home-brewed comics and scrappy artists and activists. There was also a trend toward "perzines," whose subject matter was basically just a record of the thoughts and feelings and musings of a single individual. It was a simple, idea that appealed to people's antiestablishment instincts: Like mixtapes and DIY fashion, it combined Marxist means-of-production with postmodern pop pastiche. And it was an early prototype for the sort of self-promotion that now lives online.

I had a zine, sort of. The year was 1993, the zine an "independent study" conceived by me and my best pal / roommate, Beth. We called it *Sped*, and it was a tribute to all things adolescent. It featured bratty reviews of retail stores in New York, including a scathing takedown of the customer service at Trash & Vaudeville on St. Mark's Place; a sex quiz that just asked variations on "who would you rather," revealing our early-nineties obsessions with everything from girl rockers named Kim to *The Simpsons*; and drunken marriage-proposal fan letters to "The Only Black Guy on *Class of '96*" (an ill-fated Fox show) and graphic novelist Daniel Clowes, who actually wrote us back(!); and a "recipes" section that was just the photocopied instructions from the packaging of various instafoods (Kraft Macaroni and Cheese, Top Ramen). We typed the whole thing on my old manual typewriter and distributed it to maybe four people. It had only one issue. But it was a testament and a tribute to the ideas and subject matter that fascinate me to this day: fame, music, fashion, sex, TV, MTV, and the language and community forged through women's media. In our more lucid moments (i.e., anytime we were not actually writing something for it), we would've said that *Sped* was meant to be both an example of and a commentary on zine culture: a spotlight on the cherished sense of marginalization felt by these publications' purveyors, the specificity of their interests, the rush and impermanence of popular culture, and the general impulse to connect with the like-minded through a reproducible and easily sharable medium. It was a way for us to showcase our goofy, sometimes angry, self-aware politically correct humor as well as give an outlet to our media crushes. Mostly, though, it was an excuse to get drunk and type very poorly and do stuff with scissors and glue.

And while the zine hasn't gone away (more on that in a minute), it has been largely sidelined by its younger, slicker, more popular half-sister, the blog. The obvious comparisons between these mediums abound: the self-publishing aspect, the personal element, the ability to home in on a single obsession or subculture or viewpoint or sensibility and connect to others who share said obsession. But zines had something that blogs don't: They had a guerrilla, handmade, lo-fi tactility that you just can't reproduce on the Internet. There are still some things that zine publishing just seems optimized for: comic books and other art-driven publications and anything that can hope to become a collectible. Zines appeal to young people in part because they are actual things, artifacts: They don't, as a medium, disappear behind the thing they're delivering but rather are an essential part of it.

And to me, that's what's still interesting about zine culture: It's had such a wide-ranging influence in vastly different directions, on the one hand as a direct lead-in to blogs, social media, and large-scale self-publishing; on the other, the blowing up of DIY culture, "slow" and hyper-local movements, grassroots activism, and Etsy-based retail. It's rare that something so simple and economical can embody so many valuable and important elements at once, but zines have that unusual quality and continue to inspire people to this day. It's what people nowadays would call a high-engagement medium, one that inspires loyalty and an acquisitive zeal.

So it's not all that surprising that zines have made a comeback, both in their über-indie form in places like Portland (where, as Fred Armisen and Co. assure us, the dream of the nineties is alive) and among New York's media elite, who have resurrected the medium in snazzier (but still staunchly DIY) form as a tribute to the staples-and-copier paper productions of their youth. From Condé Nasties to *Paris Review* editors, resurrecting the hallowed medium has become a thing again—one that still values first-person storytelling and the rewards of slow-paced, non-mass publishing. And beyond New York, there's growing evidence that the trend is back with a vengeance, from the zinefests throughout the world (Melbourne, San Francisco, Albuquerque, Richmond, Milwaukee) to the thriving zine collections at university libraries from Barnard to UCLA.

It's not hard to see how the enthusiasm catches on; in the course of writing this I've found my old desire to self-publish stirring again, and I've come up with a whole bunch of (mostly bad) ideas for zines I'd like to start, from a family newsletter-as-zine to a once-a-year "trends of the red carpet" digest to a perzine about my own struggles with depression. And if that sounds terrible to you, just remember: It was good enough for Ben Franklin.

THE WONDERFUL WORLD OF CATALOGS, MAGALOGS, AND CATAZINES

Y In those pre-Y2K days, a teen's most sacred day of the month was the day the dELiA*s catalog arrived in the mailbox. This was usually an after-school surprise, heavy with ritual. After acquiring a snack, one needed to drop everything, race to her bedroom, turn on the local Top 40, and spend the next hour intensely engaged with photos of pink flannel pajamas, camo messenger bags, snowflake sweaters, and so many other beautiful, beautiful things. The first reading of the catalog was rushed, a need to see everything and get a taste for this month's offerings. Then came a much more detailed and careful perusal. First, evaluating how much of your allowance could cover the cost of a pair of cargo pants. Then, building the story you'd pose to your parents in which cargo pants become your necessity—nay, an absolutely vital component for the entire family's well-being.

Most of the time this didn't work.

But still. You'd take a Magic Marker to those pages and circle everything your heart desired: frosty lipsticks, inflatable furniture, purses shaped like Chinese takeout boxes, tees and dresses laden with Hawaiian graphics.

Especially for girls living in rural areas, this was our only way to know what was cool and one of our few ways to obtain it. Marketing people *loved* us; this was a time when Gen Y buying habits started to cause shifts in the retail markets, and grown-up folks started paying attention and playing us hard. Of course, we didn't know this, but looking back, I now have to acknowledge that as much as I deemed myself an individual, no one told me what I liked more than dELiA*s. I couldn't do it for myself.

Yet the genius of dELiA*s was that there was an illusion of self-definition. Each issue featured sections with different vibes or product groupings—you'd flip through a couple of pages of cartoony graphic tees, then pastel semiformal dresses, then skater sweaters—and inevitably you'd gravitate more toward one thing than another. And because the extended part of the catalog ritual involved gushing over the pages yet *again* with your friends, you'd all have slightly different opinions. Naturally, however, everyone showed up to school three weeks later in the same sweater.

While dELiA*s was queen of the catalogs, the mid- to late nineties brought a slew of other mailbox distractions, many of which (but not all) were short-lived. There was Moxie, the skater-meets-surfer catalog that featured celebs like Rachael Leigh Cook, Jessica Biel, or Larisa Oleynik modeling clothes, and then you'd get a little interview. Similarly, there were other inventions like Just Nikki or Zoe, and people started calling them catazines or magalogs. Others you may have received: Alloy, dotdotdash, Girlfriends LA. They were like magazines, except better because there were fewer words, more pictures, and they were *free*.

Yes, these monthly gifts were about fashion for us, but in a larger sense they were about the catalogs themselves, because you couldn't have everything inside. But you could have the catalog for as long as you liked. Something compelled us to keep these issues around for months or even years—you didn't just throw them away. They always held some magic, and before their ultimate expiration, they'd be subject to diary collages, reinvented in so many other keepsake paper products.

Eventually, however, we had to throw them away, or after a number of years, they felt irrelevant. The thing is we're now all kicking ourselves for not holding on to them because they're some of the best relics of our youth and now so hard to find.

So, if you happen to have the summer '98 dELiA*s, please consider passing it along. I'd willingly wait by the mailbox all day.

SASSY, SASSY EVERYWHERE, AND NOT A BACK ISSUE LEFT ON EBAY

X I know. You've seen all the Tumblr tributes and published paeans to the greatness that was *Sassy*, and you're wondering: Does the world really need another? Maybe not. But this is happening, so I suggest we all just deal with it.

As you may have gleaned from the above-mentioned multimedia bludgeoning, lots of people from Gen X and Gen Y worship *Sassy*, the teen-magazine version of the oft-beaten Gen X dead horse known as the Candle That Burns Twice as Bright Burns Half as Long. (See also: *Freaks and Geeks,* Kurt Cobain, Nexus-6 replicants.) You've heard how much it helped so-and-so get through that seven-year awkward phase when no one understood her, or fueled what's-her-name's dreams of one day becoming an editrix (right here, folks). But for me, *Sassy*'s impact can be seen farther and wider: I believe it's been crucial to the way I've come to understand media, brands, and the workplaces that produce them.

Launched in 1988 as the American answer to Australia's highly successful teen mag *Dolly, Sassy* quickly became a bastion for smart, funny, feminist-minded discussion of pop culture and the challenges of teen life. It was, for many, the first and only place they'd read about things like STD prevention, women's rights, and the groundswell of indie music and culture coming out of places like D.C., New York, Seattle, Olympia, and Athens, Georgia. It was maligned and boycotted by right-wing organizations that objected to its frank discussion of sexual matters and shocking assertion that gay people should be allowed to exist and be in love. And the journey was short: It ended in 1994 when Petersen Publishing bought and eviscerated the brand.

This early demise just made the rest of us love it more for being impermanent, embattled, and doomed. We also, of course, loved it for everything else it was: a mash-up of traditional glossy and indie zine, a platform where underground culture and mainstream girl talk commingled to make this fun, funny, self-referential, rare, beautiful yet unstable early-nineties isotope. It taught us to take staunch, defiant positions on everything from abortion rights to Tiffani Amber Thiessen. It provided, in the form of Christina Kelly, a powerful treatise on the importance of voice, and an overall sense that their community was our community.

Indeed, one of *Sassy*'s most distinctive qualities was the way it made the reader feel like part of the editorial action: You had the feeling that the staff was pulling back the curtain to reveal the wacky office culture behind the scenes, giving us unrestricted, unmediated access to their world of bickering editors, cute indie bands, awesome skater boys, fun fashion, and complex interpersonal politics. We came to see editor-in-chief Jane as the benevolent but somewhat absent working mom, and writer Christina as the über-cool, sometimes scary big sister, who might bully you mercilessly one minute but then sneak you out for ice cream and an all-ages Sebadoh show the next. To be clear, I claim no actual knowledge of Christina or any of her *Sassy* cohort; the characters we got in the magazine version may or may not have resembled the real people they were based on. It doesn't really matter (to me, I mean); what it taught me, and a generation of women, was that you could be confused, ambivalent, worshipful, crushed out, political, angry, smart, undecided, and even self-contradictory—essentially, you could still be some evolving version of your teenage self—and still speak up, join the conversation.

This wasn't restricted to the editors. Again and again, as readers of *Sassy*, we got the strong, reassuring message that it was *us* the writers and editors cared about, it was us they wanted to hear from, and it was because of us that they came to work—even more than their BFFs Kim Gordon and Michael Stipe, even more than the cute bands and TV stars; we were the cause they rallied around, their raison d'être. And in the end I believe I entered the working world with these *Sassy*-born ideas ingrained: that really great magazines or websites or brands of any kind were ones that forged real, authentic relationships with their readers or customers, had a recognizable voice and recognized yours, and actually gave a shit. It's why I genuinely believe *Sassy*'s legacy isn't restricted to women's media. Yes, we see its impact on everyone from Tavi Gevinson to Jezebel.com, but I also see it in Zappos founder Tony Hsieh, who made his customer not his king but his bro, someone he'd always come through for; or in Target, which somehow straddles the mass/niche divide with an ease that constantly impresses; or in the way readers of Gawker and other popular sites address not the publication but individual writers directly in their comments, underscoring the notion that they feel a direct, personal relationship to the things they're reading. Was this all *Sassy*'s doing? Of course not. But in the world of 1980s and nineties media, you'd be hard pressed to find a more prescient prototype for the way many of today's successful brands interact with their audiences.

For me personally, there are and have been signs of *Sassy* everywhere. I took a lot of it with me when I found myself on a staff of smart, opinionated, beautiful, stylish, rebellious, dramatically inclined women. Because of *Sassy*, I brought with me to work the idea that a great brand, a real brand, stems from real people and real personalities. It's not something you manufacture in a conference room with the help of a consultant and a whiteboard, or find buried in a mission statement, but something to be discovered in the day-to-day operations and conversations of the people who do the work, who make the product or perform the service. And a great media brand is one where they do it not for their own sake in some solipsistic vacuum (at least on good days) but for the sake of the readers.

For all of that and many other things as well (e.g., an enduring appreciation for Marc Jacobs's grunge collection for Perry Ellis), I have *Sassy* to thank. It's why I proudly join the already deafening chorus of eulogizers in lamenting its all-too-early demise. And while I think the original staffers would agree that it's better to burn out than fade away, I will never stop wishing that there could have been a third option.

THE MYTH, THE LEGEND, THE SASSY

YThere is no such thing as a person who does not like *Sassy* magazine. If there is, they belong in a dungeon with all those other cretins who hate things like gay people and ice cream. Go back to your planet. You are not welcome.

Gen Y doesn't just *like Sassy*, its members *love Sassy*. And the same can be said of Gen X. There are a myriad of things that have driven Gen Y's and Gen X's paths to cross, but when it comes to the teen magazine that helped make the nineties the nineties, our paths don't merely meet up. They, like, do it together. (Sex.)

We are so obsessed with *Sassy* that we refuse to believe it wasn't actually made for Millennials. We ignore that we missed out, but still feign complete oneness with the brand. This is not a hard thing to do. We do this by responding with a wistful "Ooooh, *Sassssyyyy*" every time its name is mentioned, and somehow this seems to communicate an authentic empathy.

Although I can't quite pinpoint it, there must have been a moment of discovery, because our complete *Sassy* fetishization didn't exactly feel gradual. All of a sudden, *Sassy* was just there, a martyr to our generation, and we felt the compulsion to mourn collectively with our Gen X fellows, to express in all caps the sadness for its absence, to lament in frowny-face emoticons the lack of the perfect substitute.

We are, in fact, a cult.

A cult whose members are twentysomething women with Wi-Fi connections, Sassyists began by hoarding images—*Sassy* covers and photo shoots—and creating digital shrines, using Tumblr and Facebook as temples. Sassyists are unswerving in their devotion to the prophet, Jane Pratt. And they felt renewal through the arrival of an apostle: teen blogger Tavi Gevinson, who, although a member of the generation after ours, would offer us a vision of hope for the continuance of Sassyism generation after generation.

I count myself among the Gen Y *Sassy* disciples; however, I'm perhaps not orthodox or even reform. I'm more one of those "I'm culturally Sassyish, but I don't really practice or believe in the Holy Subscription." The truth is, I had never even held or read an actual issue until very recently, my sacred experiences being limited to momentary instances of revelation via Tumblr re-blogs. Even in the crossover years, when I could have potentially seen an issue of *Sassy* in the supermarket, I don't remember even registering its presence.

The thing that draws us most to *Sassy* is its myth, its legend, and its intangibility. If we were dating, *Sassy* would be playing the game just right by being so unavailable, we want her even more. But beyond this part, what are we supporting and celebrating? Maybe it's an easy aesthetic target—mixed with overlit photos, bushy eyebrows, zine-y layouts—to provide us with a snapshot of a bygone era. For moderate enthusiasts like me who follow blindly and don't actually know its content through and through, we understand that *Sassy* still stands for good, and even when our grasp is vague, we can sense the nobility it championed: individualism, revolution, creation of a new culture. Somehow, even with this small amount of information, Gen Yers have managed to create a body of beliefs. Although not explicitly written, you can imagine what it might say. *Thou shalt DIY. Thou shalt respect thy sisters. Thou shalt bleach thy hair and wear Doc Martens. Thou shalt not be lame and mainstream. Thou shalt not succumb to stupidity.*

As disciples, we're waiting for the resurrection, and there have been many false predictions about its arrival. On the occasions we've heard whiffs and rumors, we buzz with excitement. While working my first job out of college—as a Web assistant at a certain women's magazine with a penchant for putting different numbers in front of the verb "to please"—the digital team was often treated to talks and seminars with prominent Silicon Valley figures. For one of these sessions, Jeff Jarvis, a journalist and tech guru, came to talk to us about innovating on the Web. The best idea he had heard recently (this was 2008), he told us in a way that implied he was letting us in on a next-big-thing secret, had come from a young woman who was trying to relaunch *Sassy* on Facebook. A collective "oooh" of intrigue sounded in the room. He didn't describe anything else about this project other than: *Sassy*, comeback, Facebook. It was genius—or so we thought. No one stopped to ask how a "Facebook magazine" would work or what it would look like. I still don't know, and either way it sounds like a bad idea.

The thing is, *Sassy* can never come back. Some of us might love a resurrection, but many of us would hate the result, and the church would split. We would lose our foundation and create a sect of neo-Sassyists. There would be wars. Rebels would drop Twitter grenades. Insurgents would wage comment warfare. Or worse: People might just not shut up about it online. After a fight of at least a thousand years, both parties would inevitably emerge from the battle defeated, left only with our blackened hearts and souls to contend with.

So the best we can do is to keep mourning the life of *Sassy* and keep alive the devotion to this act of mourning. If we do this, we just might pass on *Sassy*'s spirit and teachings so that she may reign forever and ever.

Amen, bitches.

X MARKS THE SPOT

In a world where the term "voice of a generation" gets tossed around like Uncle Ben's at a wedding, it's hard to know exactly where (and on whom) it's going to land. But in the case of Douglas Coupland, the designation and accompanying backlash seem pretty inevitable, in retrospect at least. His first novel, *Generation X*, gave a description, a zeitgeist, a mood, and a lexicon to the disaffected post-boomer segment—then slapped a catchy name on it for good measure. What'd he expect?

For those who haven't read it, *Generation X*, published in 1991, is about three white middle-class twentysomething characters at the close of the 1980s. Narrator Andy and his two BFFs, Claire and Dag, have opted out of the mainstream for the cultural and literal desert of Palm Springs, California, where they hang out a lot, put in time at their McJobs (one of Coupland's many original coinages peppered throughout, and definitely the best), play with their dogs, and tell each other stories. Stories are the central trope of the book, which itself isn't much of one, but that's kind of the point: These are folks who feel disconnected from the grand narratives of history, the great themes, the big picture.

FAUXSTALGIA: a feigned retrospective fondness and longing for things you don't remember or never actually experienced

SCHADENNEID: [From the German *Schaden*, meaning "misfortune," and *Neid*, meaning "envy"] a feeling of envy toward other people whose "big history" tragedies (World War II, the Great Depression, Vietnam) are the defining elements in their lives

NEOLOGORRHEA: a condition suffered by Gen Xers characterized by an inability to stop making up new words to describe ever more specific phenomena

MUPPIE: middle-aged urban professional

MCSNOB: anti-intellectual snob; someone who broadcasts his or her lowbrow tastes with pride and looks down on people who "read books" or "know grammar" or "think critically"

BYRONIC DISTANCE: no distance at all; total sincerity and the tendency to take oneself very, very seriously

STRIVER'S REMORSE: common Gen X affliction; embarrassment or shame associated with one's own obvious attempts to achieve success, particularly in the corporate sphere

YOUTH GROUPIE: someone who tries to prolong his own youth by assuming the interests, hobbies, and musical tastes of the younger generation

SUBURBAN OUTFITTERS: Urban Outfitters

Without a major war or sweeping cultural movement to define them, they are at a loss for what to embrace and what to rebel against. Left to piece together some semblance of an identity from the scrap heap of American popular culture, they take turns stitching together odd little tales laced with darkness, anxiety, and longing, grasping at narrative threads to give meaning and gravitas to their lives.

People have strong opinions about this book. Those who tend not to like it fall into a bunch of different categories: people who dismiss the notion of a monolithic definition of a "generation"; people who dismiss its particular definition of said generation; people who find it dated; people who find the characters privileged and unsympathetic; people who find the writing pretentious; people who say there is no story. Those who like it tend to be people who either like or don't mind being classed together with their contemporaries; people who are just glad it's not a handbook akin to what you're reading right now; people who enjoy the early-nineties meta-pastiche of poly-era Americana; people who find Coupland's clever prose, a strange combination of melancholia and snark and longing and detachment, sort of compelling.

As for me, I'm ashamed to admit I didn't read it when it came out. In fact, I read it much later on, long after the era it documents had passed. To the me of today, *Generation X* feels like it's both about me and not about me. Chronologically, it describes a group of people who are five to ten years older than I am, and some of that age difference is felt—the apocalyptic backdrop of Cold War nuclear anxiety is something I experienced, but not into my twenties. And the idea that we don't have big historical events or cultural shifts to attach to has kind of been shattered by 9/11, the major economic recession of 2008, the election of Barack Obama, and the whole Internet thing. And while I sympathize with Andy's aimlessness and alienation and admire his refusal to go with the unholy flow of mass-mediated consumer culture, I also don't always find his rants sympathetic. At one point, while talking about the Vietnam War, he says: "... they were ugly times. But they were also the only times I'll ever get—genuine capital H History times, before history was turned into a press release, a marketing strategy, a cynical campaign tool. And hey, it's not as if I got to see much real history, either—I arrived to see a concert in history's arena just as the final set was finishing." *Oh, boohoo, so sorry you missed out on something truly emotionally scarring like a big world war.* Also, the idea that history hasn't always been marketed and mediated and cynically manipulated, that this development has somehow just sprung into being in time to victimize and disappoint our generation, seems, well, wrong. And his own description of history as spectacle, a "concert," would seem to indicate that he's bought into a lot of that very marketing.

Finally, for all the nostalgia that does occupy the book, it doesn't take the form I'm most familiar with from my own generation: the nostalgia for our own pasts and the artifacts thereof. While there are lots of pop references from eras gone by—fifties diners, forties starlets, Elvis, Mary Quant—there isn't a whole lot about the characters' own childhoods. If anything, these people seem like they're in a real hurry to distance themselves from childhood, and my experience of my own generation is of people who are obsessed with theirs.

In short, it's hard not to see these characters as essentially of a different generation than the one I belong to, and I suspect they'd say the same thing about me. Andy's description of his youngest brother, Tyler, who was probably born around the same time I was, makes it clear he views him as a member of a completely different tribe: Global Teens. These kids are relentless optimists, joiners, doers, students of fashion and fun, buyers of the cynically mass-marketed ideology of diversity and "pseudo-globalism"—playing gleefully and unconcernedly into the hands of the corporate machine. And they're entitled: "Tyler is like that old character from TV, Danny Partridge," Andy says, "who didn't want to work as a grocery store box boy but instead wanted to start out owning the whole store." Which is almost exactly the sort of thing I've been known to say about the kids of Gen Y, bringing me back to the suggestion that some of the issues explored by Coupland are specific to his generation and some are simply just a slight recasting of issues that plague *every* generation—rebellion, disillusionment, marginalization, resentment, and disdain for anyone younger.

Which isn't to say that I don't see myself in the characters or find them at times relatable. I guess what I mean is this: In the end, the things I connect with most in Coupland's story are things I think everyone who's ever been in their twenties can relate to: a yearning for meaning and connection, a solace found in the bonds of friendship, a fear of the future, a desire to be different, a desire to belong. It's those things that stuck with me the most, anyway. I think it's a book about the attenuation of adolescence, and as such is definitely about me and my friends, who've made an art form of that sort of thing. So yes, it's about Generation X. It's just about everyone else, too.

THE PERKS OF BEING A GEN YER

 In its literal interpretation, we all know "Don't judge a book by its cover" is complete and utter bullshit. The proof is that you are now reading this book, and presumably its cover is awesome, and the logical sequence of events could be described as thus: You saw the cover of this book and judged it to be awesome without knowing its contents. Bravo.

You see, some of life's best discoveries are made at surface level, and that's how I came to Stephen Chbosky's *The Perks of Being a Wallflower*. It was during one of those many evenings I'd spent at the Barnes & Noble on Eighty-Third and Broadway, and the shameful truth is that I randomly selected this book because the cover—a minimalist design with empty green space, small text, and an unassuming, sepia-toned photograph of feet at the upper right corner—felt very cool, young, and modern to me. And once I saw the book was published by MTV, I assumed it was about cool, young, modern people doing cool, young, modern things.

I was only sort of right. The characters in *Perks* are indeed young. Through letters written to an unknown recipient, we meet the protagonist, Charlie, as he's entering his first year of high school in Pittsburgh. His best friends are two upperclassmen, Sam (the type of mythical, effervescent, unattainable, haunting girl all men have loved) and Patrick, and they are indeed cool, the types of kids who are still revered even though they stray from the mainstream and get off on doing live performances of *The Rocky Horror Picture Show*.

But "modern" wouldn't quite fit the story. Of course, what makes *Perks* so special is that it speaks so universally. There's Charlie's extremely dark yet endearing persona that feels familiar no matter who you are. And Chbosky fits the ultimate coming-of-age frame brilliantly by handling all those taboo topics—suicide, drugs, homosexuality, sexual abuse—in a way that never makes the reader feel talked at. There's no doubt in my mind that *Perks* belongs to Gen Y; we've not only claimed it loudly but it was also obviously meant for us, having been released in 1999. However, Charlie and his crew are anything but Gen Y. The novel begins in 1991, making Charlie about fourteen years old, and putting his birth year at 1977: He's a solid Gen Xer. And the references that make the book's world magical belong to a different generation. Music and mixtapes are particularly essential to the plot, along with TV and movies, and these references were all dated by the time Millennials were reading: the Smiths, Fleetwood Mac, Alice Cooper, Genesis, *The Graduate, Harold and Maude, Hannah and Her Sisters.*

In the early 2000s, *Perks* became a cult phenomenon and felt like something of a secret for the lucky people who had discovered Chbosky's book. Of course, in the years following, the novel's exposure would slowly snowball, gaining attention on the multiple times schools and libraries would ban it (and of course in more recent years, gaining a huge platform with the movie version starring Hermione Granger, aka Emma Watson). But what has been clear about *Perks* from the beginning is that this book somehow saved its readers. Read interviews with the author, and you'll see, they're flooring; people have thanked Chbosky for helping them come to terms with their sexuality, abandon suicide, or get through high school alive. Although in retrospect my teenage troubles were fairly average, I suppose I'm one of those people who used *Perks* to get through high school alive, and one of the reasons was that the author actually came into my life when I was sixteen, and I was lucky enough to keep up with him from time to time.

Steve Chbosky came to my high school for our annual celebration of the written word called "Everybody Reads," which I remember thinking was an embarrassing name because hopefully this was the minimum requirement for the student body, like: *Come to our school . . . we read here!* It was a hit-or-miss lineup, mainly because we were blasé teens who were totally afraid of seeming uncool. Case in point: Calvin Trillin had come the year before, and we were horrible to him. It's one of the most embarrassing and horrible memories I now have of high school. In preparation for his visit, we read *Remembering Denny*, and we then had to write letters to Trillin to supposedly praise him for his book, but instead we were scathing. He stood in the auditorium in front of my tenth-grade class, a small group of forty or so kids, with the stack of letters in his hands and just looked like *Why am I here?*

When Steve came the year after, the discussion group was even smaller—there were fifteen or so, and maybe eight of us who had read the book—and the vibe at the beginning of the talk was even worse, not only because we were a year older and therefore even bigger assholes, but also because horrible things had happened that year. Steve's visit was a mere month after September 11. That was the first day of our junior year, and we were sitting in the classroom where many of us had first heard the news of what was going on seventy blocks south from us. The memory of it lingered for some time in spots we went through on that day. I still remember exactly what I wore on 9/11: wide-leg Gap jeans with a uniform sky-blue wash, a white safari-inspired button-up with cargo pockets at the breast, a white camisole under because it was slightly sheer, and a choker-style necklace made of silver tube beads and garnet stones.

But I also remember what I was wearing the day Steve came to our class: Vintage Lee jeans with a temperamental fly that tended to unzip at the worst moments. The Demerest Run '89 T-shirt. And one of those braided ribbon hair clips that were popular for only a few months.

My classmates' terseness actually worked to my advantage, because it turned out to be one of the most amazing moments of my high school experience, and I like to think that I managed to save what could have been a very awkward half hour by asking a million questions and one in particular that he thought was so good, he didn't have an answer.

A lot of people started reading *Perks* after that visit. And when Steve came back the next year, things were different. We didn't have much longer before college; things were better. Before he left, I gave him a mixtape, which is so utterly embarrassing because I imagine Stephen Chbosky has a dumpster full of mixtapes given to him by fans, but whatever.

STEVE'S INSCRIPTION IN MY BOOK COPY:

Leonora,

It means so much to me—your enthusiasm and support. You're a
lovely young woman and I'm so happy you like the book and Charlie.
Good luck to you and your forever and always,
Stephen Chbosky 10/16/01

What stays with me now isn't how Stephen may have managed to
save an entire generation (although yea, Steve! that's awesome!) but that his
book bridged a generational gap, and that even though Charlie essentially
went to Gen X High, we Gen Yers were able to innately relate.

There's no explaining how this is, but it seems to illustrate the point
of *X vs. Y*—that while we often don't understand each other, there are instances
of perfect, arbitrary synchronicity where we just *do*.

A FINAL WORD TO GENERATION Z

Oh God, it's over. Are you so sad? We are so sad.

If there's anything we've realized in writing this book—other than that Leo is an excellent source of *Full House* trivia, and Eve knows every pre-1985 Duran Duran lyric by heart—it's that our two generations are essentially kindred spirits in many ways. We both claim the nineties as a core of our identities, and we've both seen the Internet and digital technology transform the world. We both inherited the incomplete changes wrought by the sexual revolution and gender equality movements, and we both love *Clueless*. Finally, and perhaps most tellingly, we've both been on the receiving end of accusations by our elders of apathy, self-involvement, entitlement, and naïveté.

Turns out that, a lot of what we think we see in a particular generation is just a function of how older people see younger people. We nitpick their shortcomings, analyze their circumstances, talk incessantly about how their predecessors were nothing like them, until enough time passes that we can all step back and say, "Oh, wait, we made those mistakes, too." Which may be why, when the dust clears and we all grow up a bit, the things we most identify with our generation are not the attitudes and behaviors we exhibited as twentysomethings but the cultural relics of our childhood and adolescence. For Leo it's Lip Smackers and *Titanic*; for Eve, it's *Star Wars* and leg warmers. But while the artifacts may differ, the emotion that defines our relationships to them—and to each other—is the same: nostalgia. In short, you could argue that what defines our generations, and what makes them so similar, is our shared yearning for the popular culture of your youth.

Which makes us wonder exactly how the next generation, Generation Z, will operate with respect to such things.

Because here's the thing: The reason we have all that nostalgia is that *we lost those things* for a while. There was no Internet to constantly catalog and reference yesterday's episode of *Mister Rogers* or meme-ify *The Little Mermaid*. So when those things came back via digital media, we got the chance to rediscover them. Gen Z won't have to rediscover anything; they live in a world where nothing ever goes away. And they're often as conversant in the popular culture of years past as we are because they have access to all of it. Everything exists in the present, all the time, all at once.

Because Gen Zers have unprecedented access to information and media from both the past and present, they'll face a different sort of challenge: figuring out how to locate value in the sea of media and entertainments they've grown up in. Eve has nostalgia for *Sesame Street* because it was one of three TV shows she ever watched as a child; would she have felt the same way if her options had been effectively limitless?

We wonder if because of all of this, the next generation will challenge the idea of what a generation actually is. They may find different ways to find one another, identify themselves, and communicate about who they are and what they care about. But one thing they can definitely count on: Older folks (that'd be us) will accuse them of apathy, self-involvement, entitlement, and naïveté. Some things never change.

PHOTOGRAPHY CREDITS

Page 26: Bono (left): Helge Øverås; Bono (right): David Shankbone; **Page 27:** Liz Phair (left): ATO Records; Liz Phair (right): Capitol; Madonna (left): RexUSA; Madonna (right): iStock; Beastie Boys (left & right): Capitol; **Page 28:** Janet Jackson (left): A&M; Janet Jackson (right): Virgin; Sting (left): RexUSA; Sting (right): Yancho Sabev; Radiohead (left): Parlophone; Radiohead (right): ATO Records; **Page 41:** Christina Aguilera: Rafael Amado Deras; Mandy Moore: Susie Jay; Jessica Simpson: U.S. Government; Spice Girls: Featureflash/Shutterstock.com; Britney Spears: iStock; Backstreet Boys: Featureflash/Shutterstock.com; 5ive: RexUSA; Hanson: RexUSA; *NSYNC: Featureflash/Shutterstock.com; 98 Degrees: Featureflash/ Shutterstock.com; **Pages 44-45:** Molly Ringwald: RexUSA; Naomi Campbell: iStock; Kim Gordon: RexUSA; Sofia Coppola: Siren-Com; Kate Moss, Courtney Love, Winona Ryder: Featureflash / Shutterstock.com; Lisa Bonet: RexUSA; Claire Danes, Drew Barrymore, Jennifer Lopez, Nicole Richie, Gwen Stefani: Featureflash/Shutterstock.com; Ashley and Mary Kate Olsen: Joel Seer/Shutterstock.com; Lindsay Lohan, Beyonce: iStock; **Page 151:** iBook: Carlos Vidal; Macintosh classic: Alexander Schaelss; Kaypro II: Hstoff; Palm Pilot: Channel R; Nokia: Tomhannen; Pager: Florian Fuchs; Nintendo: David Arango

ACKNOWLEDGMENTS

This book is a direct expression of who we are, so a truly comprehensive list of thank-yous would be annoying for, well, everyone. Suffice it to say that if you've ever taught us anything interesting, encouraged us to write more things, or been Madonna, we're grateful.

Foremost, we thank our parents, Daniel Epstein and Betsey Peters Epstein, who raised us both to pursue our passions, to love art and books and humor and music, and to be good people and good siblings.

Keven McAlester, Eve's husband, and Amy Talkington, our sister-in-law, have both been hugely helpful and supportive throughout the process of writing and revising this book, reading early and late drafts and providing invaluable feedback. Deanna Kizis has likewise been a huge supporter and helpful reader (and, of course, an amazing friend).

We are indebted to and kind of totally in love with our editor at Abrams, David Cashion. From the first hour of our acquaintance with him (and with his impressive Star Wars paraphernalia collection), we knew it would be magic—and we were right. We are likewise obsessed with our agent, Brettne Bloom, at Kneerim, Williams & Bloom, whose commitment to our concept and appreciation for our voice have been constant sources of delight and support; her former colleague, Caroline Zimmerman, was hugely instrumental in shepherding our project through its early stages and a delight to work with. Deb Wood, our immensely talented designer, has been a wonderful collaborator. Thanks also to Lauren Wade for taking awesome author photos and Ashley Kucich for making us look presentable.

Additionally, Eve thanks the people who were her closest friends and mentors during her most formative Gen X years: Allegra Silbiger, Beth Lewand, Ethan Smith, S. Paige Baty, Deanna Kizis, and Jeanne Fay Manfredi. Additionally, she'd like to thank Ashley McAdams, Crystal Meers, Dany Levy, Katie Dick, Pavia Rosati, and all her former colleagues at DailyCandy who helped her to become a better and more confident writer, editor, and thinker.

Leonora would like to thank the folks who have inspired her and encouraged her to keep writing: Daniel Horowitz, Stephen Chbosky, Cecile Fenske, Laura Sumser, Drew McFadden, and Kelley Hoffman. And a huge thanks to "Geneva," "Anne," "Molly," "Lisa," "Holly," "Greg," and "Mark" (whose names have obviously been changed)— the experiences we had are why this book exists.

EDITOR: DAVID CASHION
DESIGNER: DEB WOOD
DESIGN ASSISTANCE: HEESANG LEE
ILLUSTRATIONS BY KELLY BLAIR
PRODUCTION MANAGER: ERIN VANDEVEER

LIBRARY OF CONGRESS CONTROL NUMBER:
2013945879
ISBN: 978-1-4197-0770-4

PRINTED AND BOUND IN THE UNITED STATES
10 9 8 7 6 5 4 3 2 1

ABRAMS IMAGE BOOKS ARE AVAILABLE AT
SPECIAL DISCOUNTS WHEN PURCHASED IN
QUANTITY FOR PREMIUMS AND PROMOTIONS
AS WELL AS FUNDRAISING OR EDUCATIONAL
USE. SPECIAL EDITIONS CAN ALSO BE CREATED
TO SPECIFICATION. FOR DETAILS, CONTACT
SPECIALSALES@ABRAMSBOOKS.COM OR THE
ADDRESS BELOW.

THE ART OF BOOKS SINCE 1949

115 WEST 18TH STREET
NEW YORK, NY 10011
WWW.ABRAMSBOOKS.COM